Keith Beaumont
Priest of the French Oratory

BLESSED
JOHN HENRY
NEWMAN

Theologian and spiritual guide
for our times

2 -

◆ *Portrait of Newman*
by Sir John Everett Millais, 1881

John H. Cardinal Newman

ACKNOWLEDGEMENTS

I wish to express my special thanks to members of the Association Française des Amis de John Henry Newman, of which I am currently President, for their assistance in the choice of extracts from Newman's works. The Association works towards making Newman better-known in the French-speaking world, by means of translations and studies of his work, the publication of an annual review, *Études Newmaniennes*, and biennial international conferences. Its website address is:

www.jhnewman-france.org

Heartfelt thanks go also to Fr Richard Duffield, Fr Philip Cleevely and Br Lewis Berry of the Birmingham Oratory, and to Br Daniel Varholy, for their editorial assistance, for the respective contributions of the first two to this book, and for the supply of and authorization to use photographic material.

Keith Beaumont
Oratoire de France

◆ *Newman around 1867*

- 3

PREFACE

John Henry Newman is a figure of immense significance for the Universal Church. His prophetic voice continues to speak far beyond the confines of 19th century England. Almost every issue of significance for the Church today is enlightened by reference to his spirit, life and thought. The relationship of these three elements, the spiritual, the moral and the intellectual, is at the heart of Fr Keith Beaumont's book, the official biography commissioned for the beatification.

Newman's experience in 1816, his first conversion, made him intensely conscious of the presence of God in his life. It also made him aware that how we think about God and how we live our lives are of vital importance for our faith. Holiness of heart, right belief and uprightness of life are all requirements for the faithful Christian.

This fidelity to the call of God frequently put Newman at odds with the wisdom of his own time. What can come across to us as dramatic conflicts of ideas often meant for him courageous stands and painful separations from family and friends. This was especially true in 1845 when he followed the "kindly light" of truth into the Catholic Church which he came to know as "the one true Fold of the Redeemer."

It is precisely here that Newman can be seen as a confessor of the Catholic faith, willing to suffer for the truth. Newman suffered much in his search for Catholic truth; and he suffered much in making it better understood once he had found it.

Fr Beaumont's biography gives a clear account of all the major themes of Newman's life and work. The importance of the independence of the Church from the State, the pioneering work on the development of doctrine, the role of conscience in the Christian life, the nature of faith, education, the role of the laity, his spiritual guidance: all are covered in the context of Newman's life and times.

Not least among the virtues of this biography is the judicious choice of citations from Newman's own work so that Newman's thought is in almost every case conveyed in his own words. Newman is not well served by short and selective quotation. Indeed he is often misrepresented. If in his own time Newman was frequently misunderstood, this is even more the case today. For partisans of many divergent views the power of Newman's name is often more important than what he really says. But Newman resists recruitment by any one party. Fr Beaumont not only quotes from the well-known works, but also directs us to some lesser known sources to give us a balanced and complete view of the subtlety of Newman's thought.

It is a mark of the universal significance of John Henry Newman that Pope Benedict XVI has made an exception to the usual practice and agreed to beatify Newman in person. The same universal significance can be seen symbolised in this official biography, written by an Australian priest of the Oratoire de France and destined to be read by those from the world over who will gather in September to see Newman beatified. They will find in this book an extraordinary grasp of Newman's significance and a genius for making it known. I would like to thank Fr Keith Beaumont and Les Éditions du Signe for bringing us this excellent biography and for their great efforts in making it available in good time for the beatification.

Very Rev. Richard Duffield C.O.
Provost of the Birmingham Oratory
Actor of the Cause of John Henry Newman

INTRODUCTION

John Henry Newman is one of the dominant figures in Christian thought of the last few centuries, both as a theologian and a spiritual guide. He will be beatified by Pope Benedict XVI during the latter's visit to Britain in September 2010 – the first beatification performed by Pope Benedict XVI himself, and a sign of the importance which he attaches to Newman. This beatification, it is to be fervently hoped, will soon be followed by Newman's canonisation. Many of us consider that he also deserves to be declared a Doctor of The Church.

He was at one and the same time an intellectual, a man of action, and a man of prayer. He was a prolific thinker and writer. He was one of the most influential preachers of his age. He was the leader of a movement aiming at the theological and spiritual renewal of the Church of England, which radically altered its character forever. And although he remained very discreet concerning his spiritual life, this was undoubtedly of great richness and depth.

Newman has left us a vast body of writings: he himself published 37 volumes; a dozen or so others have appeared since his death; and new, hitherto unpublished writings continue to appear! Nor should we forget the some twenty thousand letters by him which survive, which have now been published in 32 large volumes in a splendid scholarly edition.

His published work displays also an astonishing diversity: 12 volumes of sermons; numerous theological and historical studies, including a large number of essays devoted to the Church Fathers, on whom he was one of the leading experts of his day; a work on the principles of university education which continues to arouse interest and controversy; a religious autobiography; meditations and prayers; a volume of verse and a long dramatic poem, set to music by the composer Sir Edward Elgar; and finally even two novels. (When an over-enthusiastic admirer once described him, during his lifetime, as a "saint", he protested that saints did not write novels!)

◆ *Newman and Blessed Dominic Barberi*

Newman a saint?

I have nothing of a Saint about me as every one knows, and it is a severe (and salutary) mortification to be thought next door to one. I may have a high view of many things, but it is the consequence of education and of a peculiar cast of intellect – but this is a very different thing from being what I admire. I have no tendency to be a saint – it is a sad thing to say. Saints are not literary men, they do not love the classics, they do not write Tales. I may be well enough in my way, but it is not the 'high line'. [...]. It is enough for me to black the saints' shoes – if St Philip uses blacking, in heaven.

"Letters and Diaries", XIII, p. 419

Many have spoken of his influence on the Second Vatican Council. The French philosopher and friend of Pope Paul VI, Jean Guitton, called him "the invisible thinker of Vatican II". Paul VI himself saw in him an "outstanding precursor" of the Council, declaring in 1964 that "the clarity of his insights and teaching shed precious light on the problems of the Church today"[1]. Pope John-Paul II quotes him in his 1998 encyclical *Fides et ratio* as an exemplary figure in the ongoing dialogue between faith and reason. Joseph Cardinal Ratzinger, future Pope Benedict XVI, has several times stressed Newman's deep influence on his own theological thinking and on that of his whole generation. In a lecture given in 1990 entitled "Newman belongs to the great teachers of the Church", he declared that Newman's teaching on conscience and on doctrinal development constitutes "a decisive contribution to the renewal of theology". And he concluded his lecture with these words:

> The characteristic of the great doctor of the Church, it seems to me, is that he teaches not only through his thought and speech, but rather by his life, because within him thought and life are interpenetrated and defined. If this is so, then Newman belongs to the great teachers of the Church, because at the same time he touches our hearts and enlightens our thinking[2].

---

1 • Telegram to the Newman Congress of 1964, quoted in *L'Osservatore Romano*, English edition, 4 June 1970.

2 • "Newman gehört zu den grossen Lehrern der Kirche", lecture given in German originally published in *John Henry Newman, Lover of Truth. Academic Symposium and Celebration of the first Centenary of the Death of John Henry Newman*, Rome: Pontificia Universitas Urbaniana, 1991. English translation in *Benedict XVI and Cardinal Newman*, ed. Peter Jennings, Oxford: Family Publications, 2005, p. 35.

::::: THE EXPERIENCE OF 1816

Newman was born in London in 1801, the eldest of six children in a solidly middle-class family. His father was then a banker in the City, though his fortunes were to undergo a dramatic downturn and his eldest son would be obliged to support his mother and sisters and also to come to the aid of his two brothers. The family belonged, as did most self-respecting middle- and upper-class families at the time, to the Church of England, which was and still is the "Established" Church of the realm, its temporal head (or "Supreme Governor") being the sovereign and its legislation, at the beginning of the 19th century, being subject to a vote in Parliament.

◆ *Southampton Place, where Newman spent part of his early childhood*

◆ *Francis (Frank) Newman, younger brother of John Henry*

◆ *Mary Newman, John Henry's youngest sister and his favourite*

As was the case with most Anglicans at the time, the Bible occupied a central place in the life of the Newman family. Every family then possessed its own copy of the Bible, in the "King James" (or "Authorized") Version which, by the quality of its language, constitutes one of the masterpieces of English literature. The Bible was indeed the cornerstone of the religious life of the country. Newman was later to use the term "Bible religion" to designate what he called "the national religion of England in its length and breadth" which consisted "not in rites or creeds, but mainly in having the Bible read in Church, in the family, and in private" (*Grammar of Assent*, p. 56).

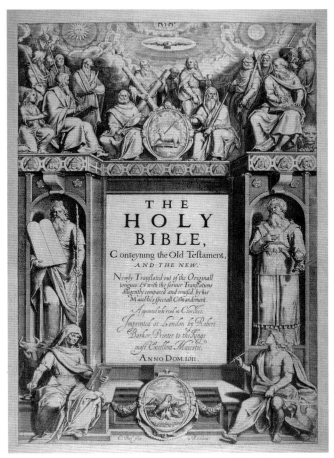

◆ *King James Bible*

The most celebrated passage in the whole of Newman's works: "myself and my Creator"

When I was fifteen, (in the autumn of 1816,) a great change of thought took place in me. I fell under the influences of a definite Creed, and received into my intellect impressions of dogma, which, through God's mercy, have never been effaced or obscured. [...] I [...] believed that the inward conversion of which I was conscious, (and of which I still am more certain than that I have hands and feet,) would last into the next life, and that I was elected to eternal glory. I have no consciousness that this belief had any tendency whatever to lead me to be careless about pleasing God. I retained it till the age of twenty-one, when it gradually faded away; but I believe that it had some influence on my opinions, in the direction of those childish imaginations which I have already mentioned, viz. in isolating me from the objects which surrounded me, in confirming me in my mistrust of the reality of material phenomena, and making me rest in the thought of two and two only absolute and luminously self-evident beings, myself and my Creator [...].

"Apologia", p. 4

From the moment he could read, thanks particularly to the influence of his grandmother and his Aunt Elizabeth, Newman became an avid reader of the Bible. Gifted with an exceptional memory, he learned whole chapters and even books by heart.

At the age of fifteen, he underwent an experience which was to shape the course of his life. He himself described it as his first "conversion". It is even, in fact, in the strict sense of the term, his *only* conversion, since the original and traditional meaning of the term does not refer to the leaving of one Christian tradition or denomination for another, but to a person's *turning towards* God. The young John Henry, still a schoolboy, encountered God not merely as an "object" of belief or thought, but as the "subject" of an overwhelming experience.

He refers to this experience and to the circumstances surrounding it – in a manner however which hides as much as it reveals – in a passage of his autobiography which constitutes perhaps the most celebrated passage in all his numerous and multifarious writings.

The concluding formula, "myself and my Creator", has given rise to endless commentaries, many of them wide of the mark and some frankly grotesque. It has been alleged that Newman is inviting us to make of our "self" a sort of cocoon in which we can shut ourselves away with "our" God. How should we interpret this formula? And why, in particular, does the author place "myself" before "my Creator"?

The explanation is quite simply that the very structure of the sentence expresses an *awakening of consciousness*. The fifteen-year-old boy becomes conscious of himself first, as a thinking, sentient and self-aware being. Then, in the intimate depths of this consciousness of self, he discovers the presence of Another, in whom he recognizes God. The young Newman's experience is analogous to that of St Augustine, expressed by the latter in the celebrated formula, "God is more intimate to me than I am to myself"[3].

---

3 • *Confessions*, Book III, 6

This experience of God as an inner Presence seems, in fact, to have been a frequent, if not constant, experience for Newman. He attributes to Charles Reding, the chief protagonist of his first novel, *Loss and Gain* (1848), the predominant "characteristic" of possessing "an habitual sense of the Divine Presence". The heroine of his second novel, *Callista* (1856), a young Greek pagan mysteriously drawn to Christianity, discovers the presence of God in her "heart". Of course, one should never totally identify the characters of a novel with its author, but it is nonetheless legitimate to see in them something of the latter. And we find indeed in Newman's *Apologia pro vita sua* words which recall those of Callista when he speaks of "this voice, speaking so clearly in my conscience and my heart".

"An habitual sense of the Divine Presence": Charles Reding in *Loss and Gain*

Charles's characteristic, perhaps above anything else, was an habitual sense of the Divine Presence; a sense which, of course, did not ensure uninterrupted conformity of thought and deed to itself, but still there it was — the pillar of the cloud before him and guiding him. He felt himself to be God's creature, and responsible to Him — God's possession, not his own.

"Loss and Gain", pp. 230-1

◆ *Loss and gain, title page*

"I feel that God within my heart": the experience of Callista

"Well," she said, "I feel that God within my heart. I feel myself in His presence. He says to me, 'Do this: don't do that.' You may tell me that this dictate is a mere law of my nature, as is to joy or to grieve. I cannot understand this. No, it is the echo of a person speaking to me. Nothing shall persuade me that it does not ultimately proceed from a person external to me. It carries with it its proof of its divine origin. My nature feels towards it as towards a person. [...] An echo implies a voice; a voice a speaker. That speaker I love and I fear."

"Callista", pp. 314-15

An inner certitude of the existence of God: extract from Newman's Apologia pro vita sua

[T]he being of a God [...] is as certain to me as the certainty of my own existence, though when I try to put the grounds of that certainty into logical shape I find a difficulty in doing so in mood and figure to my satisfaction [...]. Were it not for this voice, speaking so clearly in my conscience and my heart, I should be an atheist, or a pantheist, or a polytheist when I looked into the world.

"Apologia", p. 241.

As to the fact of calling God "my Creator", far from expressing any desire to "lay hands on" God and to place Him in his own service, Newman is suggesting on the contrary a relationship of *dependence*. Like the hero of his first novel, he recognizes himself as a "creature" of God, and desires to allow himself to be "created" – or recreated – by Him.

Noteworthy also is the fact that the boy's experience was that of God as *Absolute*. Henceforward, God would be at the centre of his life and thought. He would even place the relationship between the self and God at the heart of every fully realized human life. An extract from a sermon of 1833 recalls, both in its content and its manner, the above-quoted passage from the *Apologia*: as our religious sensibility deepens, the preacher tells us, we begin to perceive that "there are but two beings in the whole universe, our own soul, and the God who made it", and that "to every one of us there are but two beings in the whole world, himself and God".

◆ *Newman, 'The Young Rector', painting by Magar, 2009*

"There are but two beings in the whole universe, our own soul, and the God who made it"

To understand that we have souls, is to feel our separation from things visible, our independence of them, our distinct existence in ourselves, our individuality, our power of acting for ourselves this way or that way, our accountableness for what we do. These are the great truths which lie wrapped up indeed even in a child's mind, and which God's grace can unfold there in spite of the influence of the external world; but at first this outward world prevails. We look off from self to the things around us, and forget ourselves in them. Such is our state, — a depending for support on the reeds which are no stay, and overlooking our real strength, — at the time when God begins His process of reclaiming us to a truer view of our place in His great system of providence. And when He visits us, then in a little while there is a stirring within us [...]; — and we begin, by degrees, to perceive that there are but two beings in the whole universe, our own soul, and the God who made it.
Sublime, unlooked-for doctrine, yet most true! To every one of us there are but two beings in the whole world, himself and God [...].
And now consider what a revolution will take place in the mind [...], in proportion as it realizes this relation between itself and the most high God.

"The Immortality of the Soul",
PPS, I, pp. 19-21

Lastly, the references to a "definite Creed" and to "impressions of dogma" remind us that, from the time of this experience and up to the very end of his life, Newman was an indefatigable defender of "dogma". (The word has acquired in contemporary usage a pejorative sense, whereas in its original Greek usage it signified simply "thought" or "opinion".) Newman found himself confronted, in fact, by a growing tendency within contemporary "liberal" Protestantism which consisted of rejecting all clearly defined theological doctrine in favour of a largely or purely moralistic and sentimental Christianity. Not that, for Newman, "dogmas" constitute an end in themselves: if he emphasizes over and again their importance, it is because he has firmly grasped the fundamental truth that it is necessary for our ideas concerning God to be as clear and precise as is possible, since the way in which we *think* of God determines our manner of *praying* and of *relating* – or of *not* praying and *not* relating – to Him.

In the period immediately preceding and following this fundamental experience of 1816, Newman came under the influence of that form of Christianity known as "Evangelicalism". Springing from the experience and teaching of John Wesley (1703-91), an Anglican clergyman rejected by the "Established" Church who remains one of the great religious figures of modern times, the Wesleyan "revival" was beginning, in the early

◆ *John Wesley*

years of the nineteenth century, to make its influence felt more and more inside the Church of England. The chief elements of Wesley's teaching were the absolute primacy of the Bible, the importance of personal holiness, the need for a personal "conversion", and the existence of an "invisible" Church, made up solely of those living this "inner" Christianity, vastly more important than the visible and institutional Church. Its influence on Newman was deep and lasting, even if he was later to distance himself from, and to criticize sharply, certain teachings of the Evangelicalism of his own age – in particular its conception of "conversion" as a unique and sudden event characterised by intense feeling; a tendency towards introspection or even spiritual introversion (the believer examining closely the state of his own soul in order to determine whether he was or was not in a "spiritual state", the only means of acquiring the certainty of being "saved"); and, more generally, the overwhelming importance accorded to "feeling". (The Anglican theologian Henry Chadwick commented ironically that the Evangelicals of Newman's time interpreted the Lutheran doctrine of "Justification by Faith" to mean "justification by feeling"[4]!) Under the guidance of his then mentor, the Rev. Walters Mayers, an Anglican clergyman of Evangelical tendency, the young Newman read avidly a series of authors, "all of the school of Calvin". But the writer who "made a deeper impression" on his mind than any other was Thomas Scott, to whom, Newman was to admit in the *Apologia*, "(humanly speaking) [he] almost owe[d] [his] soul". It was Scott who "first planted deep" within his mind "that fundamental truth of religion" that was the doctrine of the Holy Trinity. And for years he "almost used as proverbs" what he "con-

◆ *Thomas Scott*

sidered to be the scope and issue of his doctrine, 'Holiness rather than peace' and 'Growth the only evidence of life'" (*Apologia*, pp. 4-5).

◆ *Newman around 1863*

4 • Preface to *John Henry Newman. Selected Sermons*, ed. Ian Ker, Paulist Press, 1994, p. 5

⠿ OXFORD

◆ *Trinity College*

The young Newman revealed himself very early on to be a precocious and brilliant scholar, to the extent that his father enrolled him when he was but sixteen at Trinity College, Oxford. The old Universities of Oxford and Cambridge then formed part of the Anglican "Establishment" and constituted the principal centre of formation of its clergy. Newman was to remain at Oxford, as undergraduate student and then as Fellow of Oriel College, at the time the most intellectually vibrant of the colleges making up the University, for a total of twenty-eight years, that is to say almost a third of his whole life.

But whilst pursuing an academic career, he wished also to become a clergyman – or, as Newman himself tellingly put it, a "minister of Christ". In the then Church of England, the situation of clergyman was all too frequently seen first and foremost in terms of social status and income. Newman's view was radically different: though he did not at the time see ordination as a sacrament, he saw in it a *conse-cration* of his whole life, even going so far as to speak of

♦ *Oriel College, showing Newman's rooms (middle row on right)*

his ordination "vow". Even more remarkable for an age in which lifelong clerical celibacy was virtually unheard of, he had come to believe more and more strongly ever since his conversion experience of 1816 that God was calling him to "lead a single life". He even dreamed for several years around this time of engaging in "missionary work among the heathen" (*Apologia*, p. 7).

On the occasion of his ordination as deacon, on 13 June 1824, he expressed in his private journal his feeling of henceforth "belonging" to God, and the following day added this characteristic note: "I have the responsibility of souls on me to the day of my death" (*Autobiographical Writings*, p. 201).

"I am thine, O Lord": Newman's ordination as deacon in the Church of England

It is over. I am thine, O Lord; I seem quite dizzy, and cannot altogether believe and understand it. At first, after the hands were laid on me, my heart shuddered within me; the words "for ever" are so terrible. [...] Yet Lord, I ask not for comfort in comparison of sanctification... I feel as a man thrown suddenly into deep water.

"Autobiographical Writings", p. 200

Following his diaconal ordination, Newman was appointed curate in a poor suburban parish of Oxford, St Clement's. To the amazement of all – for such zeal was rare at the time – he set about visiting *all* of his parishioners, returning several times to see the sick and the most poverty-stricken. It was not for him merely a duty: he confided to his friend Pusey that "visiting the sick" was "the most agreeable part of [his] duties" (*Letters and Diaries*, I, p. 191).

◆ *Trinity College Chapel*

◆ *Bust of Newman by Westmacott, 1841*   ◆ *St Clement's Church, Newman's first parish*

This discovery of a working-class world of extreme poverty and even destitution led him gradually to revise certain of the ideas inculcated in him by his former "Calvinist" mentors. His pastoral experience convinced him that "the religion which he had received" from the latter "would not work in a parish", that it was "unreal", and that "Calvinism" – with its division of men into two categories, the "elect" and the "reprobate" – was "not a key to the phenomena of human nature" (*Autobiographical Writings*, pp. 77-9). Around the same time, his colleagues of Oriel College set about curing the young man of his at times almost paralyzing timidity and – more importantly – of his "evangelical" ideas. The latter process, however, was to be slow and never fully completed; for Newman, while abandoning many of his evangelical ideas, would forever retain and be marked by what was best in the teaching of his Protestant masters.

In 1826 he was appointed to the post of tutor at Oriel College, charged with both lectures and – more importantly – with the personal monitoring of students. It was a task which many of his fellow-tutors carried out with a minimum of zeal, to the extent that the better motivated students felt obliged to engage, at their own expense, private tutors. Newman undertook, with the support of two of his younger colleagues, a radical revision of the whole system: the tutor must be, in his eyes, a "minister of Christ" concerned with the "spiritual good" of his students, having "the aim of gaining souls to God" and being "not a mere academical Policeman, or Constable, but a moral and religious guardian of the youths committed to him". The newly elected Provost of the College, Hawkins, did not however see mat-

ters in the same way, accusing Newman of creating a system of "mere personal influence and favouritism" (*Autobiographical Writings*, pp. 89-92). The conflict led Hawkins to refuse from 1830 onwards to allocate any new students to Newman. The progressive idleness to which the latter was condemned led him to invest his energies in new interests and activities, which would lead in time to a vast programme of renewal of the Anglican Church. The irony of the situation did not escape Newman: in his private journal, he noted that "had he not been deprived of his Tutorship", the resulting movement, "humanly speaking", "never would have been" (*Autobiographical Writings*, p. 96)!

◆ *Oriel College*

⫶⫶ DISCOVERY OF THE CHURCH FATHERS

Liberated from his tutorial duties and with time on his hands, Newman plunged into studying – in the original Greek and Latin, of course – the Fathers of the Church. He had first conceived a passion for them on reading Joseph Milner's History of the Church of Christ *in the Autumn of 1816; he read them, he tells us, "as being the religion of the primitive Christians" (Apologia, p. 7).*

Now he set about reading them systematically, in chronological order, starting with the Apologists of the second century. In a celebrated passage of the *Apologia*, he describes the sense of wonder which he experienced then; the passage reveals also his predilection for the Church of Alexandria, then one of the five great patriarchates of Christendom, and his admiration for its great archbishop and defender of the Trinitarian faith, St Athanasius.

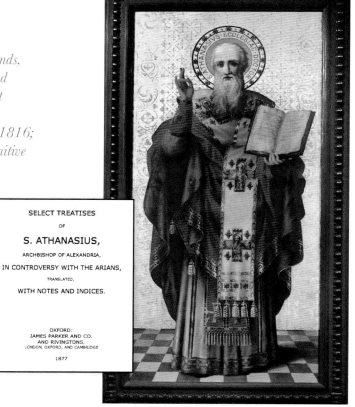

SELECT TREATISES
OF
S. ATHANASIUS,
ARCHBISHOP OF ALEXANDRIA,
IN CONTROVERSY WITH THE ARIANS,
TRANSLATED,
WITH NOTES AND INDICES.

OXFORD:
JAMES PARKER AND CO.
AND RIVINGTONS,
LONDON, OXFORD, AND CAMBRIDGE
1877

◆ *St Athanasius, Birmingham Oratory church*

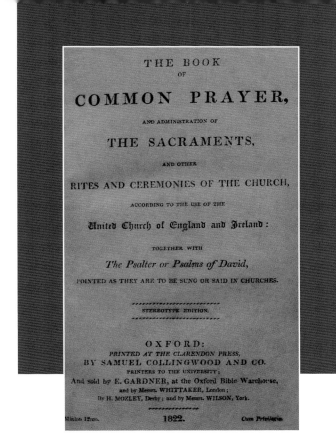

◆ *Book of Common Prayer*

Slowly but progressively this reading and study of the Fathers brought about a profound renewal in his own thinking. He discovered what he himself called the "Catholic" – that is, universal – dimension of the Church. He discovered also the importance of what he called "apostolicity", that is the rootedness of the Church in an unbroken tradition going back to the time of the Apostles themselves. The Church of England at the time, however, had lost this sense of "catholicity" and "apostolicity": it had become a merely *national* Church, which moreover considered itself as essentially "Protestant". True, there existed a tension between its two chief foundational documents, the first version of each of which went back to the mid-sixteenth century. The *Thirty-Nine Articles*, the official confession of faith of

the Anglican Church, displayed a resolutely Protestant spirit and a fierce hostility towards Roman Catholicism. *The Book of Common Prayer* (or *Prayer Book*), on the other hand, designed to be an official liturgical manual, preserved a considerable part of the liturgy inherited from the mediaeval Church. But its rubrics were widely ignored by the clergy and, apart from those provisions regarding such celebrations as baptism and marriage, had largely fallen into disuse.

::: PREACHER AT ST MARY'S

In January 1828, Newman was appointed vicar of the parish of St Mary the Virgin in the heart of Oxford, which served as both parish church and as the "official" church of the University for its solemn occasions.

It was at St Mary's that he preached – generally at Vespers on Sunday afternoons – most of the 600 or so Anglican sermons which he wrote out and carefully preserved, and of which approximately a third were published, between 1834 and 1843, in the six volumes of *Parochial Sermons* and two volumes of *Plain Sermons by Contributors to Tracts for the Times*. Slowly but steadily, this preaching attracted townsmen, students and fellows of the University. Many even came from afar in order to hear him. In the space of a few years, Newman became the most listened to, most read and most influential preacher in the whole country.

◆ *Church of St Mary the Virgin, Oxford*

According to today's criteria, as a preacher he did everything which we are told *not* to do! His sermons were long – rarely less than half an hour, and often more. He *read* a fully written-out text, without raising his eyes towards the congregation. He carefully avoided rhetorical devices and a searching after dramatic effect. He also had an extremely personal manner of speaking: he spoke rapidly, in a voice described by many as "musical", and then left long pauses between his sentences.

And yet the effect on his congregations was, by all available accounts, captivating. According to William Lockhart, who went up to Oxford in 1838, Newman's sermons had the effect of "a new revelation. He had the wondrous, the supernatural power of raising the mind to God, and of rooting deeply in us a personal conviction of God, and a sense of His Presence"[5]. The critic James Mozley, writing in 1846, noted that his "influence has been of a peculiarly ethical and inward kind". He was struck particularly by Newman's ability to empathize with his hearers: "A sermon of Mr. Newman's enters into all our feelings, ideas, modes of viewing things. He wonderfully realizes a state of mind, enters into a difficulty, a temptation, a disappointment, a grief. […]. Nay, he enters deeply into what even scepticism has to say for itself; he puts himself into the infidel's state of mind […]. Persons look into Mr. Newman's sermons and see their own thoughts in them."[6] Perhaps the most precise and detailed appreciation is that of a future professor of poetry at Oxford, J. C. Shairp, who described Newman's style and manner of preaching as sober and yet curiously exhilarating.

---

5 • *Cardinal Newman*, London, 1891, pp. 25-6.
6 • Article in the *Christian Remembrancer*, cit. R. W. Church, *The Oxford Movement. Twelve Years, 1833-1845*, 1892, pp. 139-40.

A testimony to Newman's preaching by a future professor of poetry at Oxford

The centre from which his power went forth was the pulpit of St. Mary's, with those wonderful afternoon sermons. Sunday after Sunday, year by year, they went on, each continuing and deepening the impression produced by the last. [...] About the service, the most remarkable thing was the beauty, the silver intonation of Mr. Newman's voice as he read the lessons. [...] When he began to preach, a stranger was not likely to be much struck. Here was no vehemence, no declamation, no show of elaborated argument, so that one who came prepared to hear "a great intellectual effort" was almost sure to go away disappointed. [...] The delivery had a peculiarity which it took a new hearer some time to get over. Each separate sentence, or at least each short paragraph, was spoken rapidly, but with great clarity of intonation; and then at its close there was a pause lasting for nearly half a minute; then another rapidly but clearly spoken sentence, followed by another pause. It took some time to get over this, but, that once done, the wonderful charm began to dawn on you. [...] His power showed itself chiefly in the new and unlooked-for way in which he touched into life old truths, moral or spiritual, which all Christians acknowledge, but most have ceased to feel — when he spoke of "unreal words", of the "individuality of the soul", of the "invisible world", of a "particular Providence", or again, of the "ventures of faith", "warfare the condition of victory", "the Cross of Christ the measure of the world", "the Church a home for the lonely". As he spoke, how the old truth became new; how it came home with a meaning never before felt! He laid his finger gently, yet how powerfully, on some inner place in the hearer's heart, and told him things about himself he had never known till then.

J. C. Shairp, "Keble", in "Studies in Poetry and Philosophy", 1868, p. 211

◆ *Church of St Mary the Virgin*

Newman's sermons are doctrinal or dogmatic. They set forth a high and rigorous moral ideal (without however ever descending into mere moralising). They display an acute psychological understanding, and the spiritual advice offered by the preacher is rooted in a lucid and penetrating psychology.

They are also rooted in an intimate knowledge of the Bible. Not only does Newman repeatedly quote Holy Scripture, but he possesses the novelist's art of narration and of vivid evocation of character.

A small selection of examples must suffice to illustrate these various qualities. Over and again, the preacher emphasizes the need for a personal encounter with God in the depths of our own being.

◆ *Drawing of Newman by Maria Giberne, c. 1840*

It is in the solitude of our own "heart" that we find God, for man is "never less alone than when alone"

For, as I have said, the Christian has a deep, silent, hidden peace, which the world sees not, — like some well in a retired and shady place, difficult of access. He is the greater part of his time by himself, and when he is in solitude, that is his real state. What he is when left to himself and to his God, that is his true life. He can bear himself; he can (as it were) joy in himself, for it is the grace of God within him, it is the presence of the Eternal Comforter, in which he joys. He can bear, he finds it pleasant, to be with himself at all times, — "never less alone than when alone."

"Equanimity", PPS, V, pp. 69-70

◆ *Interior of St Mary's, with the pulpit from which Newman preached*

"God alone is the happiness of our souls"

Now the doctrine which these passages contain is often truly expressed thus: that the soul of man is made for the contemplation of its Maker; and that nothing short of that high contemplation is its happiness; that, whatever it may possess besides, it is unsatisfied till it is vouchsafed God's presence, and lives in the light of it. [...]

He alone is sufficient for the heart who made it. I do not say, of course, that nothing short of the Almighty Creator can awaken and answer to our love, reverence, and trust; man can do this for man. Man doubtless is an object to rouse his brother's love, and repays it in his measure. [...] But [...] our hearts require something more permanent and uniform than man can be. [...] We may indeed love things created with great intenseness, but such affection, when disjoined from the love of the Creator, is like a stream running in a narrow channel, impetuous, vehement, turbid. The heart runs out, as it were, only at one door; it is not an expanding of the whole man. Created natures cannot open us, or elicit the ten thousand mental senses which belong to us, and through which we really live. None but the presence of our Maker can enter us; for to none besides can the whole heart in all its thoughts and feelings be unlocked and subjected.

"The Thought of God, the Stay of the Soul",
PPS, V, pp. 316-17

There is however nothing moralistic in this invitation to a personal encounter with God, even if Newman lays enormous stress on the importance of a form of spiritual "training": the need for a perpetual self-transformation which will make us the more "open" and "receptive" to this inner Presence of God. God alone, the preacher insists, can fulfil our deepest needs, emotional as well as spiritual. Newman's message is reminiscent of St Augustine's declaration that God has made us for Himself and it is only in Him that our hearts will finally find rest and repose, or of St Teresa of Avila's formula, *Dios solo basta*, "God alone is sufficient".

Newman's preaching, it has been stated, is doctrinal or dogmatic. He explores and illustrates the meaning of the great Christian dogmas, while at the same time shifting the emphasis away from the preoccupations of his contemporaries. Christian preaching at the time – and especially that of Evangelicals – saw in the Atonement the central doctrine of Christianity: emphasis was thus placed on the suffering and death of Christ, rather than on the Resurrection (whose central importance, both in Protestant and in Catholic thinking, has only been generally rediscovered in the course of the last half-century). Thanks in part to the teaching of the Church Fathers, Newman saw and emphasized the importance of the Resurrection and of the Christian's sharing, through the Holy Spirit, in the life of the Risen Christ. But he also accorded a crucial importance to the Incarnation, seeing in the presence both in us and amongst us of the Spirit of the Risen Christ a *continuation*, so to speak, of the Incarnation: Christ, having once entered this world, has in a sense never left it.

> ## Our Saviour, having once come into this world, has never left it
>
> We are able to see that the Saviour, when once He entered into this world, never so departed as to suffer things to be as before He came; for He still is with us, not in mere gifts, but by the substitution of His Spirit for Himself, and that, both in the Church and in the souls of individual Christians.
>
> *"The Indwelling Spirit", PPS, II, pp. 220-1*

He emphasizes also the importance of the doctrine of the Trinity, which for Newman, far from being a mere abstraction, expressed an experiential reality. The doctrine or dogma of the Trinity represents an attempt, in our limited human language, to express the Divine Mystery through which God *communicates* to us – by the Son and in the Holy Spirit – His own *life*. One of his favourite themes, inspired originally by St John and St Paul but confirmed many times over by the writings of the Church Fathers, is that of the "indwelling" of the Holy Spirit. The Spirit "dwells" or "lives" in us, progressively transforming our whole being and making us "partakers of the Divine Nature" (2 Pet 1: 4; King James Version). The Christian is invited to make of himself – or to allow himself to become – the "temple of the Holy Spirit".

◆ *Oriel College, with St Mary's church in the background*

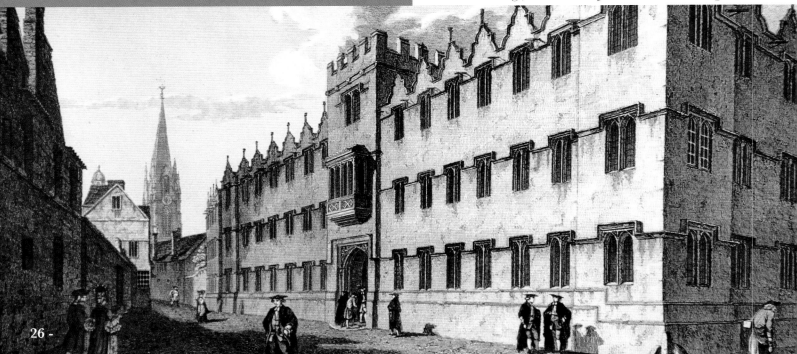

The Holy Spirit "dwells" in us "as in a temple", making us "partakers of the Divine Nature"

For instance, St. Paul says in the text, "Ye are not in the flesh, but in the Spirit, if so be that the Spirit of God dwell in you." Again, "He shall quicken even your mortal bodies by His Spirit that dwelleth in you." "Know ye not that your body is the Temple of the Holy Ghost which is in you?" "Ye are the Temple of the Living God, as God hath said, I will dwell in them, and walk in them." The same Apostle clearly distinguishes between the indwelling of the Spirit, and His actual operations within us, when he says, "The love of God is shed abroad in our hearts by the Holy Ghost which is given unto us;" and again, "The Spirit Himself beareth witness with our spirit that we are the children of God." [Rom. viii. 9, 11. 1 Cor. vi. 19. 2 Cor. vi. 16. Rom. v. 5; viii. 16.] [...]

To proceed: The Holy Ghost, I have said, dwells in body and soul, as in a temple. [...] Therefore, He pervades us (if it may be so said) as light pervades a building, or as a sweet perfume the folds of some honourable robe; so that, in Scripture language, we are said to be in Him, and He in us. It is plain that such an inhabitation brings the Christian into a state altogether new and marvellous, far above the possession of mere gifts, exalts him inconceivably in the scale of beings, and gives him a place and an office which he had not before. In St. Peter's forcible language, he becomes "partaker of the Divine Nature," and has "power" or authority, as St. John says, "to become the son of God." Or, to use the words of St. Paul, "he is a new creation; old things are passed away, behold all things are become new." [2 Pet. i. 4. John i. 12. 2 Cor. v. 17.]

"The Indwelling Spirit", PPS, II, pp. 221-3

Newman is led also, both in his theological writings and in his preaching, to reflect on the theme of "salvation". (He frequently uses the term "justification", first used by St Paul, then massively by Martin Luther and his Protestant disciples. The terms "justification" and "salvation" do not have an exactly identical meaning – the latter has a broader sense – but they share a good deal of common ground.) For contemporary Evangelicals, the "justification" or salvation effected by Christ lay essentially in a past event, his "expiatory" suffering and death on the cross. For Newman, the two terms denote a process which unfolds in the *present*: Christ saves us, each and every one individually, *here and now*, by the presence within us of His transforming Spirit, which simultaneously "saves" and "sanctifies" us.

◆ *Newman, adapted from a drawing by George Richmond, 1844*

Christ saves us, here and now, by His Presence within us

Let us never lose sight of this great and simple view, which the whole of Scripture sets before us. What was actually done by Christ in the flesh eighteen hundred years ago, is in type and resemblance really wrought in us one by one even to the end of time. He was born of the Spirit, and we too are born of the Spirit. He was justified by the Spirit, and so are we. [...] Christ Himself vouchsafes to repeat in each of us in figure and mystery all that He did and suffered in the flesh. He is formed in us, born in us, suffers in us, rises again in us, lives in us; and this not by a succession of events, but all at once: for He comes to us as a Spirit, all dying, all rising again, all living. We are ever receiving our birth, our justification, our renewal, ever dying to sin, ever rising to righteousness. His whole economy in all its parts is ever in us all at once; and this divine presence constitutes the title of each of us to heaven [...].

"Righteousness not of Us, but in Us", PPS, V, pp. 138-9

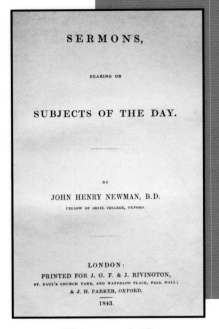

◆ *Title page of "Sermons on Subjects of the Day"*

what is wrong in the Church", once replied shrewdly: "You, and me"!)

Finally, Newman invites his listeners and readers to reflect on the very meaning of Christian life and on what it is that makes a Christian. All too often today, we are tempted to define the Christian either simply in *intellectual* terms – the Christian is a "believer", someone who "adheres" to certain "beliefs" – or simply in *moral* terms – the Christian is someone who acts in a particular way, or who attempts to live by "Gospel values". For Newman, however, true Christian life consists of *three* "dimensions": an intellectual dimension ("believing"), a moral dimension (acting according to certain "values"), and a *spiritual* dimension, in the proper and etymological sense of that much-abused term which, beginning with St Paul and throughout Christian tradition, refers to the presence and the work within us of the Holy *Spirit*. It is indeed in terms of this third "dimension" – the indwelling Presence of God, through his Spirit – that Newman sees the essential characteristic of the Christian: the "true Christian", for him, is "one who has a ruling sense of God's presence within him".

For all Newman's emphasis on the individual, however, it would be wrong to assume that he preaches a purely individualistic version of Christianity. That would be surprising, and completely contradictory, given his emphasis on the reality of the Church and on the sacraments as a "channel" of divine grace. It is simply that he insists on the fact that any collective reality must be rooted also in personal experience and action, and that there must be a connection and a coherence between the two. (Mother Teresa of Calcutta, to the question of a too-clever-by-half journalist: "Tell me, Mother,

The "heart" of every Christian "ought to represent in miniature" the universal Church

Thus the heart of every Christian ought to represent in miniature the Catholic Church, since one Spirit makes both the whole Church and every member of it to be His Temple. As He makes the Church one, which, left to itself, would separate into many parts; so He makes the soul one, in spite of its various affections and faculties, and its contradictory aims. As He gives peace to the multitude of nations, who are naturally in discord one with another, so does He give an orderly government to the soul, and set reason and conscience as sovereigns over the inferior parts of our nature. As He leavens each rank and pursuit of the community with the principles of the doctrine of Christ, so does that same Divine Leaven spread through every thought of the mind, every member of the body, till the whole is sanctified. And let us be quite sure that these two operations of our Divine Comforter depend upon each other, and that while Christians do not seek after inward unity and peace in their own breasts, the Church itself will never be at unity and peace in the world around them [...]. .

"Connexion between Personal and Public Improvement",
Sermons on Subjects of the Day, p. 132

◆ *Newman, 1844.*
From the drawing
by Richmond

A true Christian "has a ruling sense of God's presence within him"

A true Christian, then, may almost be defined as one who has a ruling sense of God's presence within him. [...] A true Christian, or one who is in a state of acceptance with God, is he, who, in such sense, has faith in Him, as to live in the thought that He is present with him, — present not externally, not in nature merely, or in providence, but in his innermost heart, or in his *conscience*. A man is justified whose conscience is illuminated by God, so that he habitually realizes that all his thoughts, all the first springs of his moral life, all his motives and his wishes, are open to Almighty God. [...]

Let us then beg Him to teach us the Mystery of His Presence in us, that, by acknowledging it, we may thereby possess it fruitfully. Let us confess it in faith, that we may possess it unto justification. Let us so own it, as to set Him before us in everything. [...] Let us acknowledge Him as enthroned within us at the very springs of thought and affection. Let us submit ourselves to His guidance and sovereign direction; let us come to Him that He may forgive us, cleanse us, change us, guide us, and save us.

"Sincerity and Hypocrisy", PPS, V, pp. 226, 235-6

Faith, reason, ethics and spiritual life: *The University Sermons*

◆ *Newman, engraving by H. Maclean made in1856, after G. Richmond's portrait of 1844*

Alongside these Sunday sermons preached by the vicar of St Mary's, Newman preached also, between 1826 and 1843, a series of fifteen "official" sermons, either in the normal course of his University duties or at the special request of the Vice-Chancellor.

These "sermons" – which are in reality lectures rather than sermons – were published in 1843 under the title of *Fifteen Sermons Preached Before the University of Oxford Between A.D. 1826 and 1843* (generally shortened simply to *University Sermons*). In them he treats of the relationship between faith and reason, between faith and morality or ethics, and between faith and spiritual life.

Newman displays an acute sense of the extreme *complexity* of every human mind, of the difficulty of describing accurately the mental processes of individuals, and of the divergences of understanding to which each is prone: "No analysis is subtle and delicate enough to represent

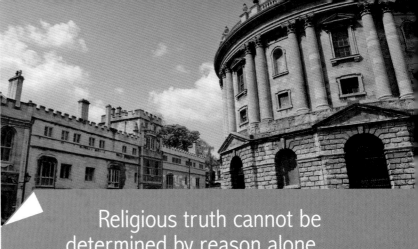

adequately the state of mind under which we believe, or the subjects of belief, as they are presented to our thoughts. […] It is probable that a given opinion, as held by several individuals, even when of the most congenial views, is as distinct from itself as are their faces" (*University Sermons*, p. 267).

He attempts to renew the contemporary debate between faith and reason by redefining each of these two terms. Faith, in so far as it attempts to construct a body of knowledge, constitutes a *form* of "reason", but one which relies on "probabilities" rather than demonstrable facts: thus reason "in this general sense […] includes of course Faith, which is mainly an anticipation or presumption". On the other hand, however, in those cases where the term "reason" designates an instrument of analysis and of verification, it is faith and faith alone which constitutes a "creative" principle, for it alone leads to *action* as opposed to mere thought: "A judge does not make men honest, but acquits and vindicates them: in like manner […] Reason analyzes the grounds and motives of actions" (*University Sermons*, p. 223), but it is faith which provides the motive for such actions.

◆ *Title page of "Fifteen Sermons Preached Before the University of Oxford Between A.D. 1826 and 1843"*

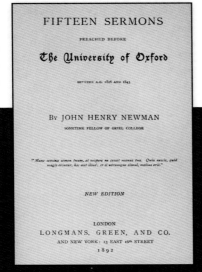

FIFTEEN SERMONS

PREACHED BEFORE

The University of Oxford

BETWEEN A.D. 1826 AND 1843

By JOHN HENRY NEWMAN

SOMETIME FELLOW OF ORIEL COLLEGE

"Manu semina semen tuum, et vespere ne cesset manus tua. Quia nescis, quid magis oriatur, hoc aut illud; et si utrumque simul, melius erit."

NEW EDITION

LONDON
LONGMANS, GREEN, AND CO.
AND NEW YORK: 15 EAST 16ᵗʰ STREET
1892

Religious truth cannot be determined by reason alone, but requires a certain inner disposition, a "preparation of the heart"

For is not this the error, the common and fatal error, of the world, to think itself a judge of Religious Truth without preparation of heart? "I am the good Shepherd, and know My sheep, and am known of Mine." "He goeth before them, and the sheep follow Him, for they know His voice." "The pure in heart shall see God;" "to the meek mysteries are revealed;" "he that is spiritual judgeth all things." "The darkness comprehendeth it not." Gross eyes see not; heavy ears hear not. But in the schools of the world the ways towards Truth are considered high roads open to all men, however disposed, at all times. Truth is to be approached without homage. Every one is considered on a level with his neighbour; or rather the powers of the intellect, acuteness, sagacity, subtlety, and depth, are thought the guides into Truth. Men consider that they have as full a right to discuss religious subjects, as if they were themselves religious. They will enter upon the most sacred points of Faith at the moment, at their pleasure, – if it so happen, in a careless frame of mind, in their hours of recreation, over the wine cup.

Sermon X, "Faith and Reason, Contrasted as Habits of Mind", University Sermons, pp. 198-9

◆ *Birmingham Oratory Church*

Faith is thus "a practical principle [...]. It is the act of a mind feeling that it is its duty any how, under its particular circumstances, to judge and to act, whether its light be greater or less, and wishing to make the most of that light and acting for the best". Yet there are always *grounds* for faith, whether a particular individual be able to state these or not: "all men have a reason, but not all men can give a reason". And a faith which remains merely "implicit", incapable of explaining or justifying itself, is in no way less real or valid than one which is "explicit": Newman the intellectual displays here and elsewhere a remarkable understanding of and sympathy for the faith of simple people, who are unable to articulate or explain their beliefs and motivations. (*University Sermons*, pp. 183, 298, 259, 253-5).

Newman repeatedly emphasizes the fact that faith involves the *whole* man and not just his intellect or his reasoning capacity. A key element in his thinking concerns the relationship between faith and our *moral dispositions*. He goes beyond the relatively superficial, if valid, assertion, that to an extent we believe (or disbelieve) what we *wish* to believe (or disbelieve). Far more important is the recognition that "faith" is not merely a matter of "adhering" to certain *ideas* or *beliefs*, but is of the nature of a *personal encounter*, or of the quest for such an encounter, or at the very least of the desire for this encounter: it thus involves what the preacher calls a "preparation of the heart". If God is indeed an inner Presence, and not a mere idea, we must engage in a process of self-transformation in order to make ourselves more *open to* and *receptive of* that Presence.

True faith leads us to "surrender" ourselves to God

What is meant by faith? it is to feel in good earnest that we are creatures of God; it is a practical perception of the unseen world; it is to understand that this world is not enough for our happiness, to look beyond it on towards God, to realize His presence, to wait upon Him, to endeavour to learn and to do His will, and to seek our good from Him. It is not a mere temporary strong act or impetuous feeling of the mind, an impression or a view coming upon it, but it is a habit, a state of mind, lasting and consistent. To have faith in God is to surrender one's-self to God, humbly to put one's interests, or to wish to be allowed to put them into His hands who is the Sovereign Giver of all good.

"Faith and Obedience", PPS, III, pp. 79-80

Finally, Newman emphasizes the relationship between faith and our *spiritual life*. As faith involves a disposition of openness to God, so God may leave an "impression" on our minds and hearts – the word being here understood in the sense of a seal which "impresses" itself on molten wax, leaving an image or a mark. It involves also a willingness to be taken "out of ourselves", in a movement towards God – whereas "the Rationalist makes himself his own centre, not his Maker; he does not go to God, but implies that God must come to him" (*Essays Critical and Historical*, I, pp. 33-34). Ultimately, faith is inseparable from hope and love: believing truly in God means *desiring* Him, *seeking* Him, placing one's *trust* in Him, and ultimately "*surrendering*" oneself to Him.

DOMVS·MEÃ·DOMVS·ORATIONIS·VOCABITVR·

The trip to Sicily
In 1833

Towards the end of 1832 Newman finished the writing of his first book, The Arians of the Fourth Century, *a wide-ranging study of the Arian heresy which denied the divinity of Christ, which divided the Christian world in the 4th and 5th centuries, and in which the author saw numerous intellectual parallels between the period studied and his own age.*

◆ *Sicilian countryside*

Exhausted by the work of research and writing, he accepted an invitation to accompany his friend Hurrell Froude and his father on a Mediterranean cruise. Fascinated by Sicily, where he was struck both by the beauty of the landscape and by the richness of the surviving remains of Greek antiquity (Sicily having then been a Greek colony), he determined to return there alone, against the advice of his two friends, after their departure for England. Alone, apart from a faithful Neapolitan manservant, in the midst of the Sicilian countryside, he fell seriously ill, possibly of typhoid fever. For a period of ten days, he lay suspended between life and death, in a state of delirium. In the midst of his ramblings, however, two

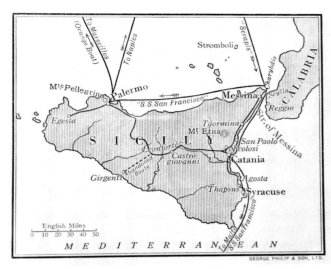

◆ *Newman's route in Sicily, from* Coram Cardinali, *by Bellasis*

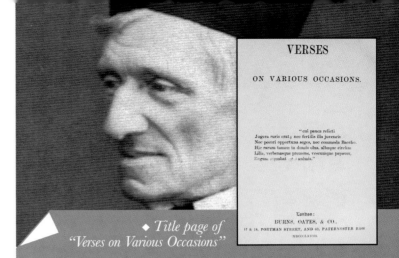

◆ *Title page of "Verses on Various Occasions"*

formulae kept recurring: "I shall not die, for I have not sinned against light, I have not sinned against light" – a statement whose precise meaning was forever to remain a mystery to him –, and "I have a work to do in England" or "God ha[s] some work for me to do in England" (*Apologia*, pp. 34-5; *Autobiographical Writings*, p. 136).

Slowly, Newman recovered. But this illness was – for the third time in his life – to bring about a new and ever-deepening "conversion", in the strict sense of the term, leading him more fully than ever to "surrender" himself to God. It coincided with a period of intense poetic creativity: it was then that he wrote the most famous of his poems, which posterity was to turn into one of the favourite hymns of all English-speaking Christian denominations. Originally entitled "The Pillar of the Cloud", a reference to the people of Israel guided by God through the Sinai desert, it is best known today by its opening words: "Lead, Kindly Light".

The Pillar of the Cloud ("Lead, Kindly Light")

Lead, Kindly Light, amid the encircling gloom
    Lead Thou me on!
The night is dark, and I am far from home –
    Lead Thou me on!
Keep Thou my feet, I do not ask to see
The distant scene – one step enough for me.

I was not ever thus, nor pray'd that Thou
    Shouldst lead me on.
I loved to choose and see my path, but now
    Lead Thou me on!
I loved the garish day, and spite of fears,
Pride ruled my will: remember not past years.

So long Thy power hath blest me, sure it still
    Will lead me on.
O'er moor and fen, o'er crag and torrent, till
    The night is gone;
And with the morn those angel faces smile
Which I have loved long since, and lost awhile.

"Verses on Various Occasions", pp. 156-7

⠿ THE OXFORD MOVEMENT

From the moment of his return to England in July 1833, Newman threw himself body and soul into a movement for the renewal of the Church of England. Though surrounded by a group of like-minded friends – in particular John Keble and Edward Pusey – he quickly emerged as the leader of the movement. Since its chief protagonists were Oxford men like himself, it has come to be known amongst historians as the "Oxford Movement".

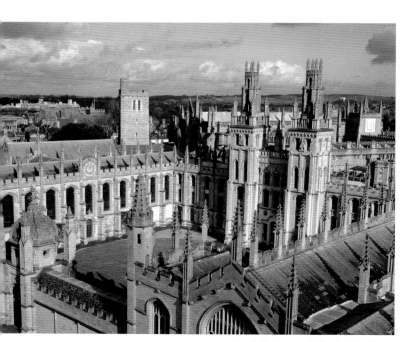

◆ *Aerial view of Oxford colleges*

The aims of the group were, in the first instance, to resist the attempts of the newly-elected Whig government to remodel the Church of England as it saw fit. But, at a far deeper level, they were to (re)awaken in that Church a consciousness of its true identity and mission. And that involved inviting bishops and clergy not only to engage in theological reflection but also to rediscover an immensely rich but largely forgotten liturgical and spiritual heritage.

It is difficult for us today to imagine the state of the Church of England in the early years of the nineteenth century. Despite isolated pockets of fervour and the existence of a small but dynamic and influential "Evangelical" current, the Church was largely characterized by spiritual torpor and doctrinal indifference. Its bishops were chosen and appointed by the government and felt bound to act in accordance with the State's policies. The chief preoccupation of a majority of its clergymen was their position in society and the income from their livings. Both bishops and clergy were seen essentially as "functionaries" of an institution, whose chief task was to preach and to carry out certain rites and ceremonies. In most parishes the Eucharist was celebrated not more than four times a year, and communion was relatively rare. The altars themselves had been removed from most churches, the central place being occupied by the preacher's pulpit. The nineteenth century, beginning with the Oxford Movement, was to see a remarkable process of rediscovery and renewal which would radically alter the face of the Church, although Anglicanism remains to this day deeply divided between mutually antagonistic tendencies.

◆ *John Keble*

The Church of England as seen by Newman in 1866

In no other institution, perhaps, have the English displayed in such a remarkable way their love of compromise in political and social matters as in the Established Church. Luther, Calvin and Zwingli, all three enemies of Rome, were equally enemies of each other. Other Protestant sects, Erastians, Puritans and Arminians, are equally distinct from and hostile towards each other. And yet it would be in no way an exaggeration to say that the Anglican Church Establishment is an amalgam of all these different varieties of Protestantism, to which a large dose of Catholicism has been added also. It is the result of the successive religious policies of Henry VIII, the ministers of Edward VI, Mary and Elizabeth, and of the influence of the Cavaliers, the Puritans, the Latitudinarians of 1688 and the Methodists of the 18th century. It has a hierarchy dating from the Middle Ages, richly endowed, enjoying an elevated social status and great political influence. The Established Church has preserved the rites, prayers and symbols of the Mediaeval Church. Its articles of faith are drawn from Lutheran and Zwinglian sources; its translation of the Bible reeks of Calvinism. […]

This remarkable Church has always been utterly dependent on the civil power, and has always gloried in that dependence. It has always regarded the power of the Papacy with fear, resentment and loathing. […]

In our own time it contains three powerful parties in which there live again the three religious principles which, in one shape or another, appear constantly throughout its history: the Catholic principle, the Protestant principle and the sceptical principle. Each of them, it is scarcely necessary to state, is violently hostile to the other two. *(Note written by Newman in 1866 for the French translation of the* Apologia. *Translated from the French.)*

In the *Apologia*, Newman states that his thinking at the time rested on three basic "principles": the "principle of dogma", with a resulting keen opposition to what he called "liberalism"; a belief in the existence of a "visible Church", to which the safeguard and transmission of its traditional teaching was entrusted, and whose sacraments were a channel of divine grace; and a fierce hostility towards "the Church of Rome" which was, since the Council of Trent (1545-63), "bound up with the cause of Antichrist". Of these three fundamental principles, only one – the third – would eventually be abandoned…

The three fundamental principles making up Newman's "position" in 1833

1. First was the principle of dogma: my battle was with liberalism; by liberalism I mean the anti-dogmatic principle and its developments. This was the first point on which I was certain. [...] From the age of fifteen, dogma has been the fundamental principle of my religion: I know no other religion; I cannot enter into the idea of any other sort of religion; religion, as a mere sentiment, is to me a dream and a mockery. As well can there be filial love without the fact of a father, as devotion without the fact of a Supreme Being. [...]

2. Secondly, I was confident in the truth of a certain definite religious teaching, based upon this foundation of dogma; viz. that there was a visible Church, with sacraments and rites which are the channels of invisible grace. I thought that this was the doctrine of Scripture, of the early Church, and of the Anglican Church. [...]

3. But now, as to the third point on which I stood in 1833, and which I have utterly renounced and trampled upon since, – my then view of the Church of Rome; – I will speak about it as exactly as I can. When I was young, as I have said already, and after I was grown up, I thought the Pope to be Antichrist. [...] in 1832-3 I thought the Church of Rome was bound up with the cause of Antichrist by the Council of Trent. When it was that in my deliberate judgment I gave up the notion altogether in any shape, that some special reproach was attached to her name, I cannot tell; but I had a shrinking from renouncing it, even when my reason so ordered me, from a sort of conscience or prejudice, I think up to 1843.

"Apologia", pp. 48-53

He describes also his state of mind at this time as being made up of confidence, of firmness, of zeal for the cause which he had embraced, and even – as he himself frankly admits – of aggressiveness, a "mixture [...] of fierceness and of sport". It was a far cry from the shy and retiring young Fellow of Oriel whom his colleagues, ten years earlier, had undertaken to bring out of his shell!

Newman's description of his state of mind on his return from Sicily and at the beginning of the Oxford Movement

I had the consciousness that I was employed in that work which I had been dreaming about, and which I felt to be so momentous and inspiring. I had a supreme confidence in our cause; we were upholding that primitive Christianity which was delivered for all time by the early teachers of the Church, and which was registered and attested in the Anglican formularies and by the Anglican divines. That ancient religion had well-nigh faded away out of the land, through the political changes of the last 150 years, and it must be restored. It would be in fact a second Reformation: – a better reformation, for it would be a return not to the sixteenth century, but to the seventeenth. [...]

Nor was it only that I had confidence in our cause, both in itself, and in its controversial force, but also, on the other hand, I despised every rival system of doctrine and its arguments too. Owing to this supreme confidence, it came to pass at that time, that there was a double aspect in my bearing towards others, which it is necessary for me to enlarge upon. My behaviour had a mixture in it both of fierceness and of sport; and on this account, I dare say, it gave offence to many; nor am I here defending it. [...] I was amused to hear of one of the Bishops, who, on reading an early Tract on the Apostolical Succession, could not make up his mind whether he held the doctrine or not.

"Apologia", pp. 43-5

◆ *Oriel College Hall*

◆ *Portrait of Edward Bouverie Pusey*

In order to disseminate his and his colleagues' ideas, Newman launched a series of polemical pamphlets to which he gave the title of *Tracts for the Times* and which was to give to the movement its other name, the "Tractarian Movement". Ninety Tracts were to be published in all, anonymously, Newman himself being the author of roughly one third. The first – in which the author (Newman) presented himself simply as a "presbyter" addressing himself to his equals – consisted of an impassioned appeal to the Anglican clergy to rediscover the true meaning of its vocation. He emphasized also the importance of the principle of "Apostolic Succession", that is, the unbroken continuity in both doctrine and Episcopal ordination since the time of the Apostles of Christ. And, turning to the then bishops of the Church of England, whose passivity and subjection to the State he deplored, he invited them with scathing irony to witness to the authenticity of their vocation by being prepared for "the spoiling of all their goods, and martyrdom"(*Tracts for the Times by Members of the University of Oxford*, London: Rivington, vol. I, 1840, p. 1.)!

The "Tractarians", as they rapidly came to be called, also published anthologies of extracts from the works of the Church Fathers and of the Anglican theologians of the 17th century (known collectively as the "Caroline divines" since most had lived around the time of the reign of King Charles I (1625-49). They were convinced that these writings contained a fullness and richness of doctrine which had since been largely forgotten. Newman himself published a much remarked-upon series of articles on "the Church of the Fathers", which was published as a book – amongst considerable controversy on account of its emphasis on the place in the Early Church of monastic life – in 1840. He also gave several series of public lectures, most notably on the meaning of "tradition" and on the concept of "justification". In these lectures

The first of the *Tracts for the Times*: an impassioned appeal to the clergy to rediscover the true sense of its vocation

Should the Government and Country so far forget their GOD as to cast off the Church, to deprive it of its temporal honours and substance, on what will you rest the claim of respect and attention which you make upon your flocks? Hitherto you have been upheld by your birth, your education, your wealth, your connexions; should these secular advantages cease, on what must CHRIST'S Ministers depend? […] There are some who rest their divine mission on their own unsupported assertion; others, who rest it upon their popularity; others, on their success; and others, who rest it upon their temporal distinctions. This last case has, perhaps, been too much our own; I fear we have neglected the real ground on which our authority is built, – our APOSTOLICAL DESCENT.

Tract I, in Tracts for the Times by Members of the University of Oxford, London: Rivington, vol. I, 1840, pp. 1-2

he sought to create a specifically Anglican theology which would constitute a *via media* or middle way between Protestantism proper and Roman Catholicism. He subsequently revised each series with a view to publication in book form: *The Prophetical Office of the Church* (1837) and *Lectures on the Doctrine of Justification* (1838). The second in particular constitutes one of his most original and profound theological works, though it was only in the second half of the 20ᵗʰ century that it was to attract the attention it deserved and to contribute ultimately to a historic agreement (1999) between Catholics and Lutherans on the subject of justification.

The most powerful vehicle for the ideas of the Movement, however, was to be found in Newman's sermons at St Mary's, preached Sunday after Sunday over a period of ten years. Not that Newman ever engaged directly, in these sermons, in polemic. But, as he admitted to his friend and mentor John Keble in a letter of 26 October 1840, he could not "disguise from [him] self" that his preaching was "not calculated to defend that system of religion which has been received for 300 years, and of which the Heads of Houses are the legitimate maintainers in this place". Even if he never "preached strong doctrine", and though most of his sermons were "on moral subjects, not doctrinal", he was nevertheless leading his hearers "to the Primitive Church if you will, but not to the Church of England" (*Letters and Diaries*, VII, p. 417).

In a series of lectures given in 1850 in which Newman addressed himself to former sympathizers of the "Movement of 1833", he suggested that a key to the understanding of the Movement lay in the formula of the Nicene Creed, "we believe in one holy catholic and apostolic Church". Each of these four epithets was the object of an ever-deepening attempt at understanding, inviting Anglicans to reflect on the links between their Church and the other historic (that is to say, the Catholic and Orthodox) Churches; to reflect on the "catholic" or universal character of the Church; on the importance or otherwise of a rich liturgical and spiritual legacy which the Church of England theoretically shared with these two other Churches, but which it had largely forgotten; and to explore the meaning of "tradition" and the existence of an organic continuity going back to the Church of the first centuries.

More than anything else, however, the dominant concern was that of "holiness". For the Oxford Movement was more than a movement of *ideas* designed to enrich Anglican theology: it was first and foremost a movement of *spiritual* renewal, through the rediscovery of the sacraments, of liturgy and of the life of prayer. Such was, indeed, the chief objective of Newman himself. More than anything else, the source of his unique influence and status as leader of the Oxford Movement lay not in developing a theory of the Church but in proposing – as a matter of practical application – a theology of *grace*.

Between 1833 and 1839, Newman was a man bounding with energy, full of passion and confidence. A wide spectrum of the provincial clergy was beginning to become excited by the new ideas. The enthusiasm of students in Oxford could be occasionally heard overflowing into the humorous slogan, "Credo in Newmanum"! And yet it was in 1839 that Newman's confidence in the cause he had so passionately espoused was, for the first time, seriously shaken.

Growing doubts about the Church of England

By dint of exploring the meaning of the ideas of "Church", "catholicity" and "apostolicity", Newman came slowly but progressively to doubt the fidelity of the Church of England to the Primitive Church, which was for him the model and point of reference.

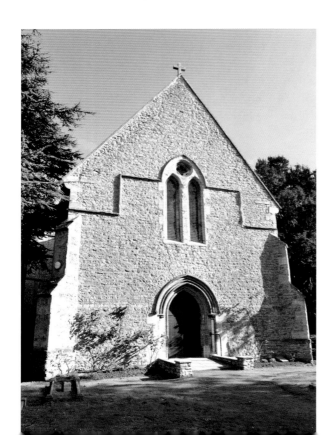

A crucial role in this process was played by his discovery of a formula of St Augustine's, *securus judicat orbis terrarum*, which Newman was to translate and expand in the Apologia in these terms: "the deliberate judgment, in which the whole Church at length rests and acquiesces, is an infallible prescription and a final sentence against such portions of it as protest and secede". These words, in the force of their impact upon his mind, he tells us, "were like the 'Tolle, lege, - Tolle, lege', of the child, which

◆ *The Anglican Church, Littlemore, built by Newman*

42 -

◆ *"The College", Littlemore*

converted St. Augustine himself". By "those great words of the ancient Father", the "theory of the *Via Media* was absolutely pulverized" (*Apologia*, pp. 116-117).

In the absence of other criteria, Newman therefore increasingly fell back, in his attempt to cling to Anglicanism, upon the criterion of "holiness", seeking signs of this in his own Church. And he threw out what was to prove to be a prophetic challenge to the Church of Rome to displays its signs of holiness, which he believed to be then sadly lacking. Indeed, he saw in the Church of Rome at this time (in part on account of his failure to understand the complex politico-religious situation in Ireland) chiefly a sinister and intriguing political body.

Gradually, the conclusion forced itself upon him that the Church of England was in a state of "schism" and that it was the Roman Catholic Church which was the true heir to what Newman liked to call "the Church of the Apostles". And this despite the fact that the Church of Rome had been for three centuries the object of a visceral hatred on the part of almost all Englishmen, as a result of the bloody conflicts of the 16th century, the memory of which was still very much alive and carefully nurtured by many.

Newman was not, however, a man to make a quick decision. On the contrary, he wished to put his growing convictions to the test. For three and a half years he lived, with a small number of companions, a quasi-monastic existence in a property he had bought and had converted into cottages and a room for his library in the village of Littlemore, some three miles from

Oxford, which was attached to his parish of St Mary's. He had always felt more at ease at Littlemore – where he had built a church and a school for the villagers – than in the "colder" and more formal atmosphere of St Mary's. Life here was now given over to study,

◆ *Newman's buildings: church, school*

> SACRED TO THE MEMORY OF
> **JEMIMA NEWMAN,**
> WHO LAID THE FIRST STONE OF THIS CHAPEL,
> JULY 21, 1835;
> AND DIED BEFORE IT WAS FINISHED,
> MAY 17 1836,
> IN THE 64 YEAR OF HER AGE.
>
> CAST ME NOT AWAY IN THE TIME OF AGE; FORSAKE ME NOT WHEN
> MY STRENGTH FAILETH ME,
> UNTIL I HAVE SHOWED THY STRENGTH UNTO THIS GENERATION,
> AND THY POWER TO ALL THEM THAT ARE YET FOR TO COME.

◆ *The memorial to Newman's mother, Jemima, who laid the foundation stone of the church at Littlemore*

to reflection, to prayer and to exercises of voluntary mortification such as fasting. Although Newman was careful to avoid using in public the word "monastery", this was nonetheless almost the first new monastic

The Catholic Church alone remains faithful to the "ethos" of the Church of the Fathers

On the whole, all parties will agree that, of all existing systems, the present communion of Rome is the nearest approximation in fact to the Church of the Fathers, possible though some may think it, to be nearer still to that Church on paper. Did St. Athanasius or St. Ambrose come suddenly to life, it cannot be doubted what communion he would take to be his own. All surely will agree that these Fathers, with whatever opinions of their own, whatever protests, if we will, would find themselves more at home with such men as St. Bernard or St. Ignatius Loyola, or with the lonely priest in his lodging, or the holy sisterhood of mercy, or the unlettered crowd before the altar, than with the teachers or with the members of any other creed. [...] And, further, it is the nearest approach, to say the least, to the religious sentiment, and what is called ethos, of the early Church, nay, to that of the Apostles and Prophets; for all will agree so far as this, that Elijah, Jeremiah, the Baptist, and St. Paul are in their history and mode of life [...] – these saintly and heroic men, I say, are more like a Dominican preacher, or a Jesuit missionary, or a Carmelite friar, more like St. Toribio, or St. Vincent Ferrer, or St. Francis Xavier, or St. Alphonso Liguori, than to any individuals, or to any classes of men, that can be found in other communions.

"Essay on Development", pp. 97-100

◆ *Cloister of "The College", Littlemore*

creation in England since the dissolution and brutal destruction of the monasteries under Henry VIII three hundred years before. And the community soon became an object of prurient curiosity and violent denunciation in newspapers and pulpits alike!

Slowly the conviction grew in Newman that the true Church was indeed that of Rome. Not that he believed the Roman Catholic Church in the mid-nineteenth century to be absolutely identical with the "Church of the Apostles", in the manner of formulation of its doctrines, in its liturgical forms and in its structures. But he became increasingly convinced that the Catholic Church, and it alone, had remained faithful to what he and his Tractarian colleagues called the "*ethos*" of Primitive Christianity – that is to say, to its basic *spiritual disposition*.

Indeed, as we shall see, Newman's decision to join the Catholic Church was based not merely on theological arguments, but on spiritual factors also.

Independently, therefore, of all theological arguments, Newman recognized in the Roman Catholic Church the form of Christian life and worship which, amongst all those that he knew, constituted most fully a vehicle of divine grace.

::: The concept of "development"

There remained, however, one major obstacle to overcome: namely, the accusation levelled by Anglicans and Protestants against the Church of Rome that she had "corrupted" the faith of the Primitive Church by "adding" beliefs and practices of which no trace could allegedly be found either in Scripture or in the early Church – for example, the invocation of the Blessed Virgin and of the saints, the "sacrificial" character of the mass, the doctrine of transubstantiation, the doctrine of purgatory, or the doctrine of papal supremacy.

At the end of 1844, Newman began therefore a new undertaking: a vast historical investigation designed to determine once and for all whether these apparent "additions" were in fact "corruptions" or – on the contrary – legitimate "developments" of elements present from the outset in Christianity but difficult to discern. The fruit of this investigation was to be *An Essay on the Development of Christian Doctrine* which would be published – in an unfinished state – at the end

◆ *Newman portrait by Sir William Charles Ross, 1845*

of 1845. For, even before he had finished writing the book, Newman had become personally convinced by the thesis he was examining.

Whilst Newman by no means invented the idea of doctrinal development, his conception of it was vastly more subtle and complex than that of any of his predecessors. He saw in it – despite the actual title of the *Essay* – a global phenomenon affecting not just doctrine but the whole life of the Church. He saw it as an inevitable, necessary and positive phenomenon. He stressed the spontaneous and – in appearance – disordered character of the process, which rendered necessary the existence of an infallible authority charged with the task of discernment. At the same time, however, he saw the process of true development as being governed by certain *laws*, and to this effect proposed a series of criteria – variously called "tests" or "notes" – enabling us to distinguish between true or authentic developments on the one hand, and "false" developments or "corruptions" on the other. Indeed, roughly two-thirds of the *Essay* is given over to outlining and illustrating these criteria, which have lost none of their relevance today.

The *Essay on the Development of Christian Doctrine* constitutes a major contribution to Christian, and in particular to Catholic, theology. In view of the historical context, it was inevitable that the work should be compared – in particular at the time of the Modernist crisis in the early years of the twentieth century – to

◆ *Title page of "Essay on the Development of Christian Doctrine"*

◆ *Charles Darwin*

Charles Darwin's *On the Origin of Species*, published just fourteen years later, in 1859. The idea of change is central to the thought of both men; but in other respects, their ideas differ radically and are almost, one might say, diametrically opposed. In the Darwinian conception of evolution, a living organism can change indefinitely, so as to possess in the end merely the most infinitesimal resemblance to its origin. For Newman, the process of development *conjugates* change and continuity, innovation and fidelity to an origin or point of departure. In a celebrated passage of the *Essay* – of which all too often, alas, only the last sentence is quoted, out of context – the author declares that if what he calls the "idea" of Christianity changes, it is *in order to remain faithful to itself.*

It is necessary, finally, to clarify what Newman means by the "idea" of Christianity which "develops" down through the centuries. The meaning of the term is often vague and even ambiguous (Newman was not always the most systematic of thinkers! But then he was breaking entirely new ground here in theological thinking…). Ultimately, the key to his thought is this: this "idea" is not a mere concept, or some kind of abstract reality, but a

The need to articulate change and faithfulness to the original "idea"

But whatever be the risk of corruption from intercourse with the world around, such a risk must be encountered if a great idea is duly to be understood, and much more if it is to be fully exhibited. It is elicited and expanded by trial, and battles into perfection and supremacy. Nor does it escape the collision of opinion even in its earlier years, nor does it remain truer to itself, and with a better claim to be considered one and the same, though externally protected from vicissitude and change. It is indeed sometimes said that the stream is clearest near the spring. Whatever use may fairly be made of this image, it does not apply to the history of a philosophy or belief, which on the contrary is more equable, and purer, and stronger, when its bed has become deep, and broad, and full. It necessarily rises out of an existing state of things, and for a time savours of the soil. Its vital element needs disengaging from what is foreign and temporary, and is employed in efforts after freedom which become more vigorous and hopeful as its years increase. Its beginnings are no measure of its capabilities, nor of its scope. At first no one knows what it is, or what it is worth. It remains perhaps for a time quiescent; it tries, as it were, its limbs, and proves the ground under it, and feels its way. From time to time it makes essays which fail, and are in consequence abandoned. It seems in suspense which way to go; it wavers, and at length strikes out in one definite direction. In time it enters upon strange territory; points of controversy alter their bearing; parties rise and fall around it; dangers and hopes appear in new relations; and old principles reappear under new forms. It changes with them in order to remain the same. In a higher world it is otherwise, but here below to live is to change, and to be perfect is to have changed often.

"Essay on Development", pp. 39-41

living source of holiness. When Newman speaks of the living "idea" of Christianity, he is referring not just to the *thought* of Christ present in men's *minds* (though it is doubtless on account of this that he uses the term "idea"), but also, and above all, to the very *Person* of Christ living both in the hearts of individual Christians and in the whole liturgical and sacramental life of the Church – the Church itself being both "sacrament" and "mystical body" of Christ, and thereby a vehicle of divine Grace.

Forms may and do change; but it is this continuous *spiritual Presence* which constitutes the ultimate criterion of all authentic "development". And any reduction of Christianity, whether it be in Newman's time or in our own, to a mere set of "ideas" or "values" — that is to say, to its purely intellectual and moral or ethical dimensions – is a sure and certain sign, to use Newman's own terminology, of a "*false* development" or "corruption".

◆ *Newman's library at the Birmingham Oratory*

::: THE CONVERSION OF 1845

As the month of October, 1845, approached, Newman set about making the final preparations for the step which had now become inevitable. He wrote to the Provost of Oriel College resigning his fellowship.

O n 7th and 8th October – though he did not post these letters until after the event – he wrote also to numerous friends to warn them that he was about to be received into the "one fold" or "one true Fold" of Christ, the Redeemer. Several members of his community at Littlemore had already been received into the Catholic Church. Through the intermediary of one of these, Dalgairns, Newman had invited Father Dominic Barberi, a Passionist priest then engaged in missionary work in England, by whose personal holiness he had been vividly struck, to come to Littlemore whilst passing through Oxford. Father Dominic arrived on the evening of 8th October, his clothes drenched as a result of having travelled for several hours on the upper deck of a stagecoach in driving rain. He was standing in front of a blazing fire drying his clothes when Newman entered the room, knelt before him and asked him to hear his general confession prior to receiving him into the Catholic Church. As the confession continued well into the night, Fr Dominic suggested that they both go to bed and resume in the morning. On 9th October, Newman completed his confession, formally abjured his Anglican faith, was given conditional baptism, and was then received, along with two other members of his community, into the full communion of the Roman Catholic Church.

◆ *Blessed Dominic Barberi*

This event was to trigger off a wave of conversions in England, mostly in intellectual circles: in the course of the next few years, several hundred former Oxford and Cambridge men left the Church of England for that of Rome. Such was the impact of Newman's action that he is still considered even now, in the English-speaking world, as *the* emblematic figure of the "convert".

This being so, it is all the more important to determine the precise nature of this "conversion". Many Catholics then hailed Newman's conversion in a spirit of triumphalism, seeing in the event a radical break between the Anglican and the Catholic Newman. The reality is far more complex.

It is true that, on a *personal* level, the event constituted in Newman's life a dramatic and extremely painful break: he lost the vast majority of his former Anglican friends; his own family disowned him; he lost his prestigious and well-paid position as a fellow of Oxford; and he was to find himself a virtual outcast from English society for almost twenty years. Indeed, in personal terms, Newman's conversion represented for him a terrible sacrifice.

But at the same time the event displays, on an intellectual and spiritual plane, a deep *continuity*. His embracing of Roman Catholicism must be seen as a continuation and culmination of his first "conversion" of 1816 and of that in Sicily in 1833. The evolution of his thought throughout the period of the Oxford Movement provides an outstanding example – to use Newman's own terminology – of "development", that is of continuity and fidelity in the midst of change. Not that his discovery of Catholicism was complete in 1845: he himself admitted that it had been an essentially intellectual process, involving few contacts with Catholics themselves and little or no exposure to the concrete reality of Catholic worship. Indeed, a source of delight in becoming a Catholic was the discovery of the "extraordinary privilege" of having Christ present in the tabernacle, and of the nature of Catholic worship in which he saw an example of "real" religion as distinct from a religion of mere words and ideas.

Yet at the same time, it can be confidently asserted that Newman, on becoming a Catholic, brought with him into the Church what he considered to be the best in both the Evangelicalism of his early years and the traditions of "High Church" Anglicanism – inserting these elements into a broader, richer and more complete whole, as he himself testifies both in the *Apologia* and in his private correspondence.

Newman's insistence on the continuity in his thought at the time of his conversion

I was not conscious to myself, on my conversion, of any change, intellectual or moral, wrought in my mind. I was not conscious of firmer faith in the fundamental truths of Revelation, or of more self-command; I had not more fervour; but it was like coming into port after a rough sea [...].

"Apologia", p. 238

The contribution of Newman's youthful Evangelicalism to his Catholicism

I will not close our correspondence without testifying my simple love and adhesion to the Catholic Roman Church [...]; and did I wish to give a reason for this full and absolute devotion, what should, what can I say, but that those great and burning truths, which I learned when a boy from evangelical teaching, I have found impressed upon my heart with fresh and ever increasing force by the Holy Roman Church? That Church has added to the simple evangelicalism of my first teachers, but it has obscured, diluted, enfeebled, nothing of it — on the contrary, I have found a power, a resource, a comfort, a consolation in our Lord's divinity and atonement, in His Real Presence, in communion in His Divine and Human Person, which all good Catholics indeed have, but which Evangelical Christians have but faintly.

Letter of 24 February 1887 to George T. Edwards, secretary of the London Evangelization Society, in "Letters and Diaries", XXXI, p. 189

huge number of letters requesting both theological and spiritual guidance. He replied systematically to each and every one, always trying to take into account as far as was possible the specific, concrete circumstances of each correspondent.

Now, in these days of greater mobility such spiritual direction is generally carried out through direct, face-to-face contact, which leaves behind no record of its content. Newman's direction, on the contrary, leaves just such a record – for our delight and edification. Many a passage of his sermons and letters enables us, in fact, to see something of the advice he gives on many and varied subjects and in a diversity of situations.

The sermons moreover reveal a marked evolution. The early ones still display traces of the "Calvinistic" influence of his early mentors and show signs of a certain rigidity. Progressively, however – although Newman never ceases to condemn in the strongest terms all forms of sin –, his thinking shows greater flexibility. As a Catholic and as founder in England of the Oratory of St Philip Neri, he took as his patron saint and model the figure of St Philip whose humanity was *transformed* by the presence in him of the Holy Spirit; yet Philip lost none of his human traits, including his sense of humour and his many eccentricities. Thus we are able, in studying Newman's teaching and advice, to speak both of a keen (and at times stringent) spiritual *realism*, and of an authentic *spiritual humanism*, both of these last two terms being given the full force of their meaning.

Newman invites us, in fact, to rediscover Christian life as a form of "spiritual training". Morality or ethics is not simply a struggle against sin, in ourselves and in the world around us, nor simply a means of doing good. It involves also a constant process of *self-transformation*, in every single one of our thoughts and deeds, in order to

◆ *Newman's private chapel in his bedroom, with portrait of St Francis of Sales above the altar*

make us more "open" and "receptive" to the presence of God in us.

The need to rediscover a conception of Christian life as a form of spiritual "training"

Further, reading in Scripture how exalted the thoughts and spirit of Christians should be, we are apt to forget that a Christian spirit is the growth of time; and that we cannot force it upon our minds, however desirable and necessary it may be to possess it; that by giving utterance to religious sentiments we do not become religious, rather the reverse; whereas, if we strove to obey God's will in all things, we actually should be gradually training our hearts into the fulness of a Christian spirit.

"Obedience, a Remedy for Religious Perplexity",
PPS, I, pp. 232-3

He emphasizes over and over again the need, for this purpose, of *self-knowledge*. True, he recognizes the difficulty we experience in really knowing ourselves; but self-knowledge is a necessary path towards the knowledge of *God*.

Just as he is aware of the complexity and individuality of each and every human being, so too he recognizes that "God deals with us very differently", that "He can bless the most unpromising circumstances" and that "He can even lead us forward by means of our mistakes".

The need for self-knowledge

Strange as it may seem, multitudes called Christians go through life with no effort to obtain a correct knowledge of themselves. [...]

When I say this is *strange*, I do not mean to imply that to know ourselves is easy; it is very difficult to know ourselves even in part, and so far ignorance of ourselves is not a strange thing. But its strangeness consists in this, viz. that men should profess to receive and act upon the great Christian doctrines, while they are thus ignorant of themselves, considering that self-knowledge is a necessary condition for understanding them. Thus it is not too much to say that all those who neglect the duty of habitual self-examination are using words without meaning. The doctrines of the *forgiveness* of sins, and of a new *birth* from sin, cannot be understood without some right knowledge of the nature of sin, that is, of our own heart. We may, indeed, assent to a form of words which declares those doctrines [...]. Yet nothing is more common than for men to think that because they are familiar with words, they understand the ideas they stand for. [...]

Now (I repeat) unless we have some just idea of our hearts and of sin, we can have no right idea of a Moral Governor, a Saviour or a Sanctifier, that is, in professing to believe in Them, we shall be using words without attaching distinct meaning to them. Thus self-knowledge is at the root of all real religious knowledge; and it is in vain,——worse than vain,——it is a deceit and a mischief, to think to understand the Christian doctrines as a matter of course, merely by being taught by books, or by attending sermons, or by any outward means, however excellent, taken by themselves. For it is in proportion as we search our hearts and understand our own nature, that we understand what is meant by an Infinite Governor and Judge; in proportion as we comprehend the nature of disobedience and our actual sinfulness, that we feel what is the blessing of the removal of sin, redemption, pardon, sanctification, which otherwise are mere words. God speaks to us primarily in our hearts. Self-knowledge is the key to the precepts and doctrines of Scripture. The very utmost any outward notices of religion can do, is to startle us and make us turn inward and search our hearts; and then, when we have experienced what it is to read ourselves, we shall profit by the doctrines of the Church and the Bible.

"Secret Faults", PPS, I, pp. 41-3

God deals very differently with each of us

God deals with us very differently; conviction comes slowly to some men, quickly to others; in some it is the result of much thought and many reasonings, in others of a sudden illumination. [...] some men are converted merely by entering a Catholic Church; others are converted by reading one book; others by one doctrine. They feel the weight of their sins [...]. Or they are touched and overcome by the evident sanctity, beauty, and (as I may say) fragrance of the Catholic Religion.

"Faith and Doubt", Discourses Addressed to Mixed Congregations, p. 233

[God] can bless the most unpromising circumstances; He can even lead us forward by means of our mistakes; He can turn our mistakes into a revelation; He can convert us, if He will, through the very obstinacy, or self-will, or superstition, which mixes itself up with our better feelings, and defiles, yet is sanctified by our sincerity.

"Private Judgment", Essays Critical and Historical, II, p. 342

In an age when the Church hierarchy was chiefly concerned with the *number* of "converts", Newman refused to pressurize those who sought advice, encouraging them to advance each at his or her own pace, and inviting them to make use of their own natural gifts or, as he put it, of the means which God had given to them. (As a result, he was at times accused of being only "half a Catholic" or of having "Protestant sympathies"!)

He refused also to impose on individuals particular forms of piety, writing for example to one lady troubled by certain "devotions" then in vogue in the Catholic Church: "It is no sin to feel it difficult to accommodate your mind to certain things, and it is better not, in the way of devotions, to force yourself at all" (Letter of 14 January 1865 to Lavinia Wilson, *Letters and Diaries*, XXI, p. 387).

He advised another lady correspondent, tormented by perplexity and doubt, to continue calmly to fulfil the duties imposed on her by her station in life, which would help her to remain confident in God's assistance, adding that God "does not call you to join the Church till you know it is the Church" (Letter of 30 August 1869 to Magdalena Helbert, *Letters and Diaries*, XXIV, p. 323).

Writing to the daughter of a friend full of questions concerning her faith, without in any way minimising the importance of intellectual arguments he invited her to "interrogate" her own "heart", in search of "the God who dwells there".

◆ *Newman around 1880*

- 89

◆ *Saint Philip Neri*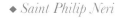

An invitation to seek God in our own "heart" and "conscience" in which He "dwells"

Another thought which I wish to put before you is, whether our nature does not tell us that there is something which has more intimate relations with the question of religion than intellectual exercises have, and that is our conscience. [...] To gain religious starting points, we must [...] interrogate our hearts, and (since it is a personal, individual matter,) our own hearts, — interrogate our own consciences, interrogate, I will say, the God who dwells there.

Letter of 25 June 1869 to Louisa Simeon,
"Letters and Diaries", XXIV, pp. 275-6

Newman was convinced of the importance of *time* and *growth* in all spiritual matters. Writing to a former pupil of the Oratory School who had just entered the Cistercian monastery of Mount St Bernard Abbey, whilst congratulating him on this step he also warned him that it was impossible for him to "know in a short time whether it is God's will that [he] should have so high a vocation" as that to which he aspired. He alerted the young man also to the possibility of an eventual over-reaction brought on by disappointment, should health problems interfere with this vocation, and advised him to "pray *now*" for the "perseverance" of which he would have need in twenty years time! (Letter of 20 March 1878 to Justin Sheil, *Letters and Diaries*, XXVIII, p. 331).

◆ *Newman with Lewis Bellasis*

◆ *Newman at work in his study*

Like all great spiritual masters, Newman emphasized also the importance of *humility*. This fundamental Christian virtue is little valued, and all too often misunderstood, in our contemporary culture of self-assertion, and is often confused with humiliation whereas it is in reality the exact opposite of the latter. Humility consists first of all in an effort to be absolutely lucid as well as rigorously honest concerning ourselves; it involves recognizing the existence in all of us of a wish to dominate over others; and then, in a pitiless and never-ending struggle, to overcome all will to power and domination, to give up all searching after personal "glory", and ultimately even all forms of self-seeking. Newman finds an example of such humility in his patron saint, Philip Neri, whom he recommends to others as a model.

The importance of humility: extract from a sermon on St Philip Neri

But I would beg for you this privilege, that the public world might never know you for praise or for blame, that you should do a good deal of hard work in your generation, and prosecute many useful labours, and effect a number of religious purposes, and send many souls to heaven, and take men by surprise, how much you were really doing, when they happened to come near enough to see it; but that by the world you should be overlooked, that you should not be known out of your place, that you should work for God alone with a pure heart and single eye, without the distractions of human applause, and should make Him your sole hope, and His eternal heaven your sole aim, and have your reward, not partly here, but fully and entirely hereafter.

"The Mission of St. Philip Neri",
Sermons Preached on Various Occasions, p. 242

At the same time, however, in an era deeply marked by the influence of a Jansenist mentality which saw an opposition between grace and nature, Newman reiterated the traditional teaching of Catholic theology expressed in the formula *gratia perfecit naturam* – grace is not opposed to nature and does not seek to destroy it in order to prevail, but works *through* nature, slowly and progressively transforming it from within. Such is the conclusion of an early chapter address to his Oratorian brothers, given in June 1848.

"Let grace perfect nature": extract from an address by Newman to his Oratorian brothers

Aim to be something more than mere University men, such as we have all been. Let grace perfect nature, and let us, as Catholics, not indeed cease to be what we were, but exalt what we were into something which we were not. Do not throw away these advantages, which God has given you, but perfect them for his service and cherish, aim at having a profound sense that these advantages are gifts not graces, talents to be improved, loans from the author of all good, for which we shall have to give an account on the last day.

"Newman the Oratorian", p. 221

The means employed by God to make a saint out of a sinner

Such are the means which God has provided for the creation of the Saint out of the sinner; He takes him as he is, and uses him against himself: He turns his affections into another channel, and extinguishes a carnal love by infusing a heavenly charity. Not as if He used him as a mere irrational creature, who is impelled by instincts and governed by external incitements without any will of his own [...]. I have already said, it is the very triumph of His grace, that He enters into the heart of man, and persuades it, and prevails with it, while He changes it. He violates in nothing that original constitution of mind which He gave to man: He treats him as man; He leaves him the liberty of acting this way or that; He appeals to all his powers and faculties, to his reason, to his prudence, to his moral sense, to his conscience: He rouses his fears as well as his love; He instructs him in the depravity of sin, as well as in the mercy of God; but still, on the whole, the animating principle of the new life, by which it is both kindled and sustained, is the flame of charity. This only is strong enough to destroy the old Adam, to dissolve the tyranny of habit, to quench the fires of concupiscence, and to burn up the strongholds of pride.

"Purity and Love", Discourses Addressed to Mixed Congregations, pp. 71-2

In the same vein, refusing to see "holiness" or "sanctity" purely in moral terms and as the fruit of man's unaided efforts, Newman rightly presents it as the fruit of the work of the *Holy Spirit* within us. But if the action of God is primordial, man must willingly *allow* God to work within him: his freedom remains entire. Thus, he reflects on the manner in which God works in order to make a saint out of a sinner.

Finally, he recognizes – not without a touch of wry humour – that we advance towards God even by means of our *mistakes* and our *failures*, and that we "walk to heaven backward".

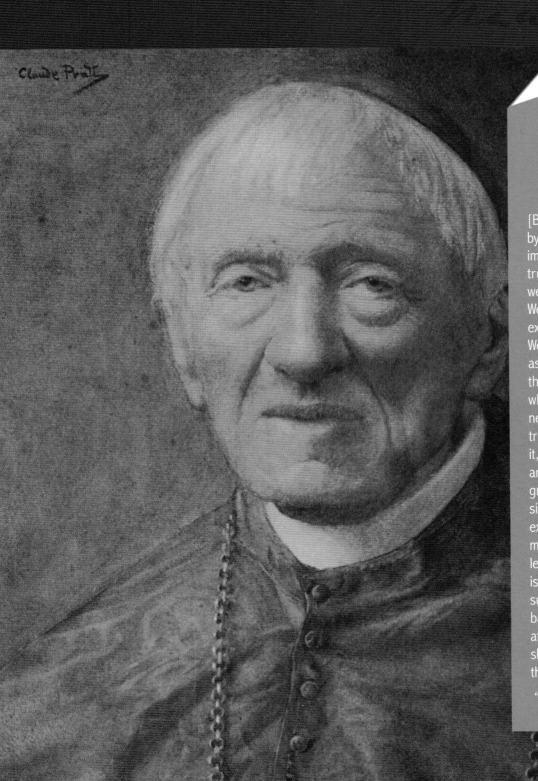

Claude Pral

We advance towards God even by means of our mistakes and failures

[B]y sinning, by suffering, by correcting ourselves, by improving, [we] advance to the truth by experience of error; we succeed through failures. We know not how to do right except by having done wrong. We call virtue a mean, — that is, as considering it to lie between things that are wrong. We know what is right, not positively, but negatively; — we do not see the truth at once and make towards it, but we fall upon and try error, and find it is not the truth. We grope about by touch, not by sight, and so by a miserable experience exhaust the possible modes of acting till nought is left, but truth, remaining. Such is the process by which we succeed; we walk to heaven backward; we drive our arrows at a mark, and think him most skilful whose shortcomings are the least.

"The State of Innocence", PPS, V, pp. 107-8

⠿ THE FINAL YEARS

The last years of Newman's life were spent peacefully at his Oratory in Birmingham. He continued to correspond, for as long as his fingers were able to hold a pen, with a host of friends and enquirers. He continued also to receive many letters of thanks and many tributes, including even tributes from a number of Protestant clergymen some of whom actually asked for his blessing. One of the very last letters received was from a clergyman who described himself as belonging to an "Independent" Church separated by an "ecclesiastical gulf" from Newman's own, yet who declared that it was through reading the latter's Parochial and Plain Sermons *that "the mind of Jesus Christ" had been "communicated" to him, and who called down upon the author the blessing of God.*

More and more during these years, Newman lived out a spirituality of "surrender" to God, based on a total and absolute confidence in Him. We have already seen evidence of this in the prayer "Lead, Kindly Light", and other examples abound. He was convinced that God had "created

◆ *Portrait of Newman, 1890*

A tribute received from a Protestant clergyman in the last months of Newman's life

If I were to allow in myself a perfectly free and natural expression of feeling, I should say with a feeling of grateful tears about my heart — 'God bless you Cardinal Newman, God bless you!' [...]

I feel that I have very inadequately stated my experience of benefit, but that precious and profound doctrine which you teach us viz: that the best part of the Christian life remains hidden, leads me to hope that from this very impoverished utterance you may be able to understand how rich and, I hope, lastingly rich you have made me in that inner life according to which we are accepted.

Letter of 7 June 1890 from W. Wood,
"Letters and Diaries", XXXI, p. 295

◆ *Newman's gravestone in the cemetery at Rednal*

[him] to do Him some definite service", and that he had a "mission" to fulfil even though he may not "know it in this life" but "be told it in the next". What he believed concerning himself, however, he believed also concerning all men: God had a mysterious "mission" for each and every one. For that reason, declared Newman, he would "trust" Him absolutely and "surrender" himself unconditionally to His will (*Meditations and Devotions*, p. 301).

At the same time, he who has often — and unjustly — been reproached with a lack of interest in social and political affairs, sought assiduously to come to the aid of hundreds of poor, mostly Irish, families living in the environs of the Oratory — most often with such discretion that it was only following his death that his Oratorian brethren discovered the full extent of his involvement. Newman's charitable activity, and the discretion with which he exercised it, offer a further parallel with his patron saint, Philip Neri.

Newman died finally, laden with honours, at the age of 89, on 11 August 1890 — the object of a deep veneration and love on the part of the vast majority of people in the English-speaking world, of all Christian denominations. Tens of thousands of mourners lined the streets as the funeral cortège passed by. He was buried in the cemetery adjacent to the Oratory's country

An expression of total "surrender" to God

Therefore I will trust Him. Whatever, wherever I am, I can never be thrown away. If I am in sickness, my sickness may serve Him; in perplexity, my perplexity may serve Him; if I am in sorrow, my sorrow may serve Him. My sickness, or perplexity, or sorrow may be necessary causes of some great end, which is quite beyond us. He does nothing in vain; He may prolong my life, He may shorten it; He knows what He is about. He may take away my friends, He may throw me among strangers, He may make me feel desolate, make my spirits sink, hide the future from me — still He knows what He is about.

"Meditations and Devotions", pp. 301-2

house at Rednal, then a village near Birmingham, in the same grave as his former friend Ambrose St John. In accordance with his own express wish, respected by his Oratorian brethren, the simple wooden coffin was covered with a form of "mould" designed to speed up the process of decomposition[7]: Newman wished, out of humility, to disappear rapidly. Is not such humility a sign of true holiness?

◆ *The brass cardinal's cross recovered from Newman's grave*

In what, finally, does the unity of Newman's life and work consist? The complexity, subtlety and wide-ranging character of his thought are such that any attempt to place him in the service of one or other "ideological" cause is both dishonest and doomed to failure. Thus the author of a masterly biography of Newman is able to state that his mind is "characterized not by contradictions but by complementary strengths, so that he may be called, without inconsistency, both conservative and liberal, progressive and traditional, cautious and radical, dogmatic yet pragmatic, idealistic but realistic"[8]. In those cultures which tend to think spontaneously in "dualistic" terms or in terms of conflicting "opposites" ("left"/"right", "progressive"/"traditionalist", etc.), Newman can be of great avail by helping us to overcome such divisions and by bringing us back to a sense of the "real". One can say of him also what he himself said of the Anglican author Thomas Scott, whose writings had left such an imprint on his mind during his youth: in his "bold unworldliness and vigorous independence of mind", Scott "followed truth wherever it led him" (*Apologia*, p. 5).

Above all else, however, the unity of Newman's life and thought is to be found in his unending search for and unconditional love of God. This great scholar and intellectual was first and foremost, as the title of a book by Cardinal Jean Honoré beautifully expresses it, "a man of God"[9]. He was a man whose life was centred upon God, who was conscious of the Presence of God within him, a man in love with God, seeking to deepen ever more that love. This key feature of Newman's life and mind can be seen in hundreds of prayers, meditations and passages of sermons. Let us conclude by several prayers which bear witness to it.

◆ *Memorial plaque in the cloister of the Birmingham Oratory church*

7 • See *Letters and Diaries*, XXXII, Appendix 11, p. 654.

8 • Ian Ker, *John Henry Newman. A Biography*, Oxford University Press, 1990, reissued 1999, p. viii.

9 • Jean Honoré, *John Henry Newman, un homme de Dieu*, Paris: Éditions du Cerf, 2003.

10 • Prayer adapted, for her own use and that of the Missionaries of Charity, by Mother Teresa of Calcutta.

Three prayers of Newman

God, the Blessedness of the Soul

To possess Thee, O Lover of Souls, is happiness, and the only happiness of the immortal soul! To enjoy the sight of Thee is the only happiness of eternity. [...] What can give me happiness but Thou? If I had all the resources of time and sense about me, just as I have now, should I not in course of ages, nay of years, weary of them? Did this world last for ever, would it be able ever to supply my soul with food? [...] Thou alone, my dear Lord, art the food for eternity, and Thou alone. Thou only canst satisfy the soul of man.

"Meditations and Devotions", p. 327

An Act of Love

My Lord, I believe, and know, and feel, that Thou art the Supreme Good. And, in saying so, I mean, not only supreme Goodness and Benevolence, but that Thou art the sovereign and transcendent Beautifulness. I believe that, beautiful as is Thy creation, it is mere dust and ashes, and of no account, compared with Thee, who art the infinitely more beautiful Creator. [...] And therefore, O my dear Lord, since I perceive Thee to be so beautiful, I love Thee, and desire to love Thee more and more. Since Thou art the One Goodness, Beautifulness, Gloriousness, in the whole world of being, and there is nothing like Thee, but Thou art infinitely more glorious and good than even the most beautiful of creatures, therefore I love Thee with a singular love, a one, only, sovereign love. Everything, O my Lord, shall be dull and dim to me, after looking at Thee. There is nothing on earth, not even what is most naturally dear to me, that I can love in comparison of Thee. And I would lose everything whatever rather than lose Thee. For Thou, O my Lord, art my supreme and only Lord and love.

"Meditations and Devotions", pp. 331-2

Jesus the Light of the Soul

How can I keep from Thee? For Thou, who art the Light of Angels, art the only Light of my soul. Thou enlightenest every man that cometh into this world. I am utterly dark, as dark as hell, without Thee. I droop and shrink when Thou art away. I revive only in proportion as Thou dawnest upon me. Thou comest and goest at Thy will. O my God, I cannot keep Thee! I can only beg of Thee to stay. "Mane nobiscum, Domine, quoniam advesperascit." [...] Remain with me till death in this dark valley, when the darkness will end. Remain, O Light of my soul, jam advesperascit! [...] Shine on me, O Ignis semper ardens et nunquam deficiens! — "O fire ever burning and never failing" — and I shall begin, through and in Thy Light, to see Light, and to recognise Thee truly, as the Source of Light. Mane nobiscum; stay, sweet Jesus, stay for ever. In this decay of nature, give more grace.

Stay with me, and then I shall begin to shine as Thou shinest: so to shine as to be a light to others. The light, O Jesus, will be all from Thee. None of it will be mine. No merit to me. It will be Thou who shinest through me upon others. O let me thus praise Thee, in the way which Thou dost love best, by shining on all those around me. Give light to them as well as to me; light them with me, through me. Teach me to show forth Thy praise, Thy truth, Thy will. Make me preach Thee without preaching — not by words, but by my example and by the catching force, the sympathetic influence, of what I do — by my visible resemblance to Thy saints, and the evident fulness of the love which my heart bears to Thee[10].

"Meditations and Devotions", pp. 364 -5

THE BEATIFICATION MIRACLE

∷ ∷

Having completed two of the four years of formation required for ordination to the Permanent Diaconate, Jack Sullivan developed a serious back problem.

In early June 2000 Sullivan had a CAT scan at the Jordan Hospital in Plymouth, Massachusetts (USA), which revealed deformities in his spinal discs and vertebrae, and spinal herniation causing severe stenosis in both legs. The CAT scan explained why Sullivan was experiencing such debilitating pain in his back and legs. He could walk only with great difficulty, hunched over and with his head facing the ground.

The new academic year would restart on September 5; and between May and August the following year (2001), as part of his preparations for ordination, Sullivan was scheduled to do an internship at a Boston hospital. As the CAT scan revealed, however, his condition would almost certainly require immediate surgery and an extended period of recuperation. It was clear to Sullivan that he would have to pull out of his formation programme.

On 26 June he was flicking through various TV channels and came upon a programme on EWTN (Eternal Word Television Network) about the Venerable John Henry Cardinal Newman. Sullivan says he had heard of Newman, but knew very little about him. The EWTN programme explained that there was a Cause in progress to have Newman canonised, and that anyone who had experienced healing through his intercession should contact the Provost of the Oratory in Birmingham (UK), the community of priests which Newman himself had founded in 1848.

Sullivan explains that after watching this programme "I felt a very strong compulsion to pray to Cardinal Newman with all my heart".

Sullivan didn't pray to Newman precisely for healing, but for "greater persistence and courage" to help him through to ordination.

Immediately, he explains, he "experienced a new and uplifting sense of trust and confidence". Sullivan says that, there and then, he knew "deep in my heart that something would happen as a result of my supplication to Cardinal Newman".

The following morning he awoke virtually pain free and with his mobility all but restored. "The joy of that first moment", he recounts, "filled my heart with gratitude to God for the intercession of Cardinal Newman."

The consequences for Sullivan of his prayer to Newman were dramatic. He was able to begin the new academic year in September 2000 and follow his classes all the way through to the end of April the following year.

Yet as an MRI scan in July 2000 disclosed, there had been no change in Sullivan's underlying condition. When, in October, Sullivan had his initial consultation with one of the USA's leading spinal surgeons, Dr Robert Banco at Boston's New England Baptist Hospital, he was told that, given his underlying condition, there was no medical explanation for the freedom from pain and level of mobility he enjoyed. Dr Banco, indeed, told Sullivan that deterioration was inevitable, and accordingly scheduled surgical intervention for December. But the intervention never took place, because Sullivan's freedom from pain continued inexplicably for almost ten months, until late April 2001.

Throughout this period, Sullivan was of course making daily prayers to Cardinal Newman.

Then on April 22 2001, just before his final class, Sullivan explains that "as suddenly as the pain had left me, it returned" In fact, he tells us, it "was more excruciating and debilitating than it was the previous summer".

Dr Banco authorised another MRI scan for May 15. The scan once again confirmed that there had been no change whatsoever in Sullivan's underlying condition since the previous July. In June, a doctor who was giving him a steroid injection said that his condition was the worst that he had ever seen.

Following Sullivan's consultation with him on May 18, Dr Banco wrote in his medical notes that "I have no medical explanation for why he was pain free for so long a time ... his pathology did not at all change, but his symptoms (pain) improved drastically".

Yet now, just as inexplicably, the pain had returned, worse than before.

Banco said that surgery was essential, and initially it looked as if nothing would be possible until October. Sullivan was praying constantly to Newman for day by day help towards ordination. On the Solemnity of SS Peter and Paul (June 29) Banco unexpectedly telephoned Sullivan to say that he would be able to operate, much earlier than envisaged, on August 9.

Even so, Sullivan's preparations for ordination once again seemed doomed. He had some 25 hours of internship to complete, before starting his final year of classes at the beginning of September. Just as he had the previous summer, Sullivan foresaw that surgery and an extended recuperation would make both impossible.

And yet, Sullivan believed, Cardinal Newman's intercession had already enabled him, when all had seemed lost, to complete his third year of studies and make substantial progress with the 120 hours of internship required of him.

To Dr Banco's astonishment, Sullivan managed to survive the summer of 2001 without further serious damage to his spine. Surgery (laminectomy) took place as scheduled on August 9 and there were complications (significant tearing of the membrane around the spine - the *dura mater*). In the following days, Sullivan was confined to bed with such severe pain that morphine had to be injected every few hours. Eventually he began physiotherapy. On August 14, Sullivan explains, "the physiotherapist gave me a walker and I somehow managed to get out of bed. The pain was so severe that after a short time I had to be helped back onto the bed by two attendants." He was told that his recuperation would take anything between eight months and a year to accomplish.

On August 15 Sullivan underwent a further session of physiotherapy:

I found it excruciatingly painful just to move onto the right side of my bed. Even with [the physiotherapist's] help it took more than five minutes. At times I had to stop and catch my breath the pain was so severe ... I finally twisted myself over the bed with my legs touching the cold floor. I had to stop in this position with my elbows and forearms supporting me on the bed.

"Silently, but fervently" Sullivan prayed to Newman:

I will never forget the simple words I said that morning: "Please Cardinal Newman, help me to walk so I can return to my Diaconate classes and be ordained."

And then, he recounts, very suddenly

I felt a very warm sensation all over my body and a sense of real peace and joy. I began to shudder and felt a very strong tingling sensation, which gripped my entire body. It lasted for what seemed a very long time, and was very strong. Then I felt a surge of strength, confidence and a tremendous sense of peace and joy that I could finally walk, and I was completely free of the crippling pain.

That morning, immediately following his prayer to Newman, Sullivan discarded the walker which the physiotherapist had given him and walked up and down the corridor outside his room, unassisted except by a cane which he needed for support after being so long in bed. He walked up and down a flight of stairs, again unassisted. "From that moment, on the Feast of the Assumption 2001, to this day", Sullivan explains

the pain has never once returned and I continue to walk normally with no restrictions and with full mobility.

Discharged from hospital on the same day, August 15, Sullivan was given painkillers "just as a precaution". He took them that night, for the first and last time. "Since that moment", he says, "I have never needed to take any further medication."

On the strength of his extraordinary healing from pain and immobility, Sullivan completed his internship in the late summer of 2001, and resumed his classes in mid-September. Having studied throughout his final academic year, he was ordained a Permanent Deacon on September 14 2002, the Feast of the Exaltation of the Cross, in Boston Cathedral (USA). On the very same day, without knowing that it was the day of his ordination, the Provost of the Birmingham Oratory emailed Sullivan to tell him that his healing had been officially judged by the Church to be worthy of further investigation.

Almost 7 years later, on July 3 2009 (the Feast of St Thomas the Apostle) the Vatican announced that the Holy Father had authorised the Congregation for the Causes of Saints to promulgate a Decree attributing a miraculous healing to

The Servant of God John Henry Newman, English Cardinal and Founder of the Oratories of St Philip Neri in England (1801-1890).

The miraculous healing in question was Jack Sullivan's, and the Church was announcing that on the basis of Sullivan's healing Newman was to be declared Blessed.

Back in October 2001, under two months after his healing, Sullivan had had a consultation with his specialist Dr Banco, who became the first authoritatively to express the miraculous character of Sullivan's recovery. On that occasion Banco had told Sullivan:

Your recovery is unbelievable, 100 per cent and totally remarkable. I have never seen a healing process occur so quickly and so completely ... I have absolutely no medical explanation to give you as to why your pain stopped. The MRI scans and the subsequent intrusive surgery confirmed the severity of your spinal condition. With the tear in your dura mater your condition should have been much worse. I have no medical or scientific explanation for you. If you want an answer, ask God.

It was then that Sullivan decided to write to the Birmingham Oratory, recounting the healing which he unreservedly attributed to Newman's intercession. This letter to the Oratory initiated the Church's protracted and painstaking examination of Sullivan's conviction that Newman is indeed his "intercessor and special friend".

A Tribunal in Sullivan's home Archdiocese of Boston gathered evidence relating to his healing at sessions running from June 2005 until September 2006. The material was judged to be of sufficient force to send to Rome, for examination and adjudication at the highest level.

In such cases the Vatican deploys two distinct scrutinies: the first medical, the second theological. The purpose of the first (medical) scrutiny is to establish, under examination by medical experts in the relevant field, whether a putative healing is genuinely inexplicable in the light of contemporary medicine. If this analysis is positive, the second (theological) scrutiny is intended to determine whether the inexplicable healing is genuinely miraculous: in other words, whether it can be safely regarded as originating in the heavenly intercession of the person to whom it is attributed (in Sullivan's case, the intercession of Cardinal Newman).

On April 24 2008, the Vatican's medical experts agreed unanimously that Sullivan's healing was indeed medically inexplicable, as Dr Banco had testified. In September 2008 the case was accordingly passed to the theologians for their assessment. After an extremely thorough examination, by the end of April 2009 they had reached unanimous agreement that Sullivan's healing could safely be judged an authentic miracle worked through the intercession of John Henry Newman.

With both medical and theological validations in place, Sullivan's cure was next considered in early June 2009 by the Cardinals and Bishops of the Congregation for the Causes of Saints, who unanimously recommended that it be passed to Pope Benedict XVI for his approval. It was this approval which, as we have seen, was announced by the Vatican on July 3 2009.

Let the last word on his miraculous healing be given to Jack Sullivan himself:

Since [the miracle] Newman has become a significant part of my life ... I have developed a very real relationship with Cardinal Newman in frequent prayer and I try to pass on what marvellous gifts I have received to those I meet ... Despite all the pain and anxiety that I have experienced throughout these eventful years it has been a deeply spiritual and enriching experience. As a result I have tried to develop a greater degree of trust and confidence in God's merciful providence, surrendering myself to his will day by day.

Fr Philip Cleevely C.O.